APPALACHIA'S LAST STAND

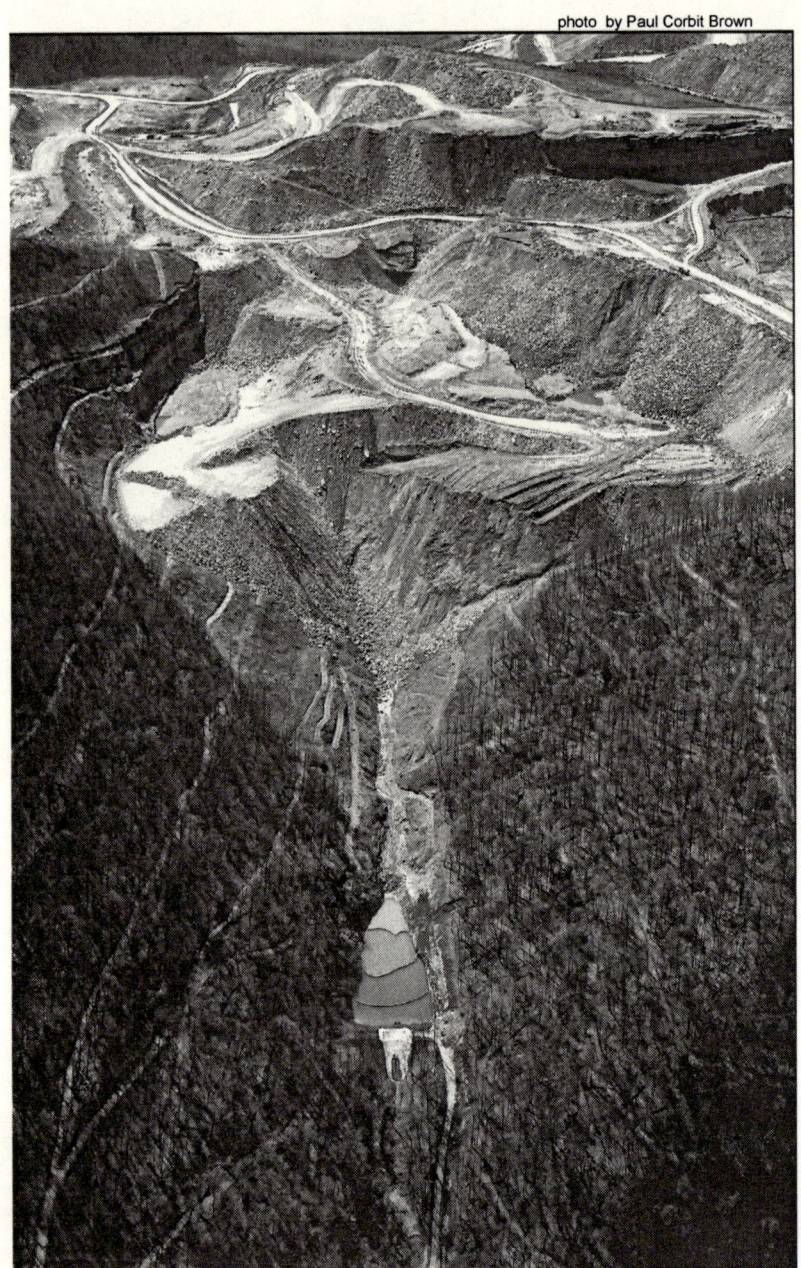

photo by Paul Corbit Brown

Appalachia's Last Stand

The Appalachian Mountains Must Not Be Sacrificed for Cheap Energy

Compiled by an Appalachian Consortium
of Writers and Photographers
in conjunction with the Alliance for Appalachia
and other organizations dedicated to
the preservation of Appalachia

Delilah F. O'Haynes, Managing Editor and Contributor
Edwina Pendarvis, Coordinating and Line Editor
Vivian Stockman, Project Coordinator and Contributor

Consultants: Chris Green, Irene McKinney and Beth Wellington
Group Contributors: Katie Fallon, Denise Giardina,
Jeff Mann, Sam L. Martin
Technical Support: Albert Perrone

Front Cover Photo by Jonathan Bolt
Back Cover Photo by Kent Kessinger

WIND PUBLICATIONS

Appalachia's Last Stand. Copyright © 2009 by Wind Publications. Printed in the United States of America. All rights reserved. No part of this book may be reproduced in any manner except for brief quotations embodied in critical articles or reviews. For information, address Wind Publications, 600 Overbrook Drive, Nicholasville, KY 40356.

Printed in the United States of America.

International Standard Book Number 978-1-893239-97-5
Library of Congress Control Number 2009936822

First edition

Thanks to the following organizations:

Coal River Mountain Watch , Kentuckians For The Commonwealth, Ohio Valley Environmental Coalition, Save Our Cumberland Mountains, West Virginia Highlands Conservancy, Appalachian Citizens Law Center, Appalachian Voices, Appalshop, Heartwood, MACED, Sierra Club Environmental Justice Program, 16 Blocks Magazine, Friends of the Mountains, United Mountain Defense, West Virginia Environmental Council, Sludge Safety Project, I Love Mountains, Stop Mountain Top Removal, Voices For Appalachia, Southwings, and the Committee for Constitutional and Environmental Justice

Contents

Foreword, *Paul Corbit Brown*	1
Introduction, *Delilah F. O'Haynes*	3
Contacts for Information and Involvement	8
Appalachia's Last Stand: An Open Letter to West Virginia Citizens and the Congress of the United States	9
Appalachia's Last Stand: The People Speak	12
Buffalo Creek: Two Stories, *Tanya Adkins and Patty Adkins*	13
Testimonies of Buffalo Creek, *Appalachian Voices*	16
Revelations 11:18, *Tanya Adkins*	19
A True Story of Bears, Mountains, and a Way of Life, *Diane Bady*	20
This Summer's Story—Voices of Those Hurt by MTR, *Shannon Bell*	22
We Are Ready for Clean Energy, *Citizen Action*	24
Super Fly (Ash)? Super *Bad*: The Cumberland Park Project, Part 1, *Garrett Bobb*	27
Kicking Ash! And Taking Names: The Cumberland Park Project, Part 2, *Garrett Bobb*	31
Conversation, West Virginia, *taped and transcribed by Delilah F. O'Haynes*	35
My Neighbor Has a TV in His Garage, *Dave Cooper*	47
Climate Change Denial, *Dave Cooper*	50
Appalachian Regional Reforestation Initiative, *Dave Cooper*	53
Sago, *Tom Donlon*	56
Morning Glories, *Katie Fallon*	57
Weapons, *Katie Fallon*	59
The Whole World is Watching—National Magazine & French TV Shine Spotlight on Mountaintop Massacre, *Laura Forman*	63

From "Like Walking onto Another Planet," *Jim Foster*	65
Christians for the Mountains, *Denise Giardina*	66
This Land Will Never Be for Sale, *Larry Gibson*	68
Paw Paw, *Stephen Godfrey*	75
My Life Is on the Line, *Maria Gunnoe*	76
Two Letters, *Jewele Haynes*	86
Four Voices from *The Herald Dispatch* – Letters	88
Appalachia – America's Fourth World, *Chris Irwin*	92
4:20 Poetry, *Jimbo*	97
Mountain Truth, *Janet Keating*	99
Almost Heaven, Not Almost Flattened, *Laura Lambert*	100
Valleys Damned, *P.J. Laska*	107
Tour of Kayford Mountain, *Jeff Mann*	108
Three Crosses, *Jeff Mann*	110
Grandpa's Place, *Sam L. Martin*	112
Ode to the Mountains, *Debra May-Starr*	113
My Family in West Virginia, and how MTR Changed It, *Whitney Miller*	115
Mourning Mountains, *an anonymous deer hunter*	117
The Character of Mountains, *Delilah F. O'Haynes*	119
Rendering Appalachia, *Delilah F. O'Haynes*	121
Highland Whisper, *Delilah F. O'Haynes*	123
Tennessee Dam Break: Another Message for Clean Energy, *Delilah F. O'Haynes*	125
Letters in Daily Mail *from The Ohio Valley Environmental Coalition Newsletter*	128
Counting Crosses, *T. Paige*	131
Mountaintop Removal: An Outsider's View of a Growing National Tragedy, *Suzanne Rebert*	132
Through the Eyes of a Child, *Tashina Savilla*	135
An Open Letter to Governor Manchin, *Mark Schmerling*	136

Mountain Air, *Marlene Simpson*	140
The Heart of Me, *Marlene Simpson*	141
A Right to Have Rights, *Juanita Sneeuwjagt*	144
One Artist's View, *Wilma Lee Steele*	151
A Day in the Life of the Walk for the Mountains, *Vivian Stockman*	153
Mountaintop Removal, *Vivian Stockman*	158
Statement of James Tawney, *taped and transcribed by Delilah F. O'Haynes*	164
Mountaintop Removal, *Seth Taylor*	169
Testimony: Charleston, West Virginia, *taped and transcribed by Delilah F. O'Haynes*	173
Destruction, *Kayla Ward*	185
This Land is God's Land, *Kayla Ward*	186
Buffalo Creek Remembered, *Ken Ward, Jr.*	188
Reclamation, *Rhonda Browning White*	191
West Virginia Forward and Back, *Rhonda Browning White*	193
The Twilight of Twilight? by *Michael Workman, Jr.*	194
Like the Mountains Richly Veined, *Marianne Worthington*	195

— Photographs —

Paul Corbit Brown – frontispiece, 8, 26, 157
Bob Gates – 85, 93, 106, 130
Buffalo Creek Flood and Disaster – 17
Maria Gunnoe – 77, 79, 81
Kent Kessinger – ix, 113, 116, 124, 155, 166, 192, 201
Kentuckians For The Commonwealth – 49, 91
Delilah O'Haynes – 4, 12, 23, 67, 70, 84, 85, 87, 96, 134, 152

Juanita Sneeuwjagt – 146
Elizabeth Spencer – 28, 32
Vivian Stockman – 39, 51, 60, 62, 74, 104, 109, 163, 184
Tennessee Mountain Defense – 30, 58, 126
U.S. Geological Survey – 14
Kayla Ward – 102

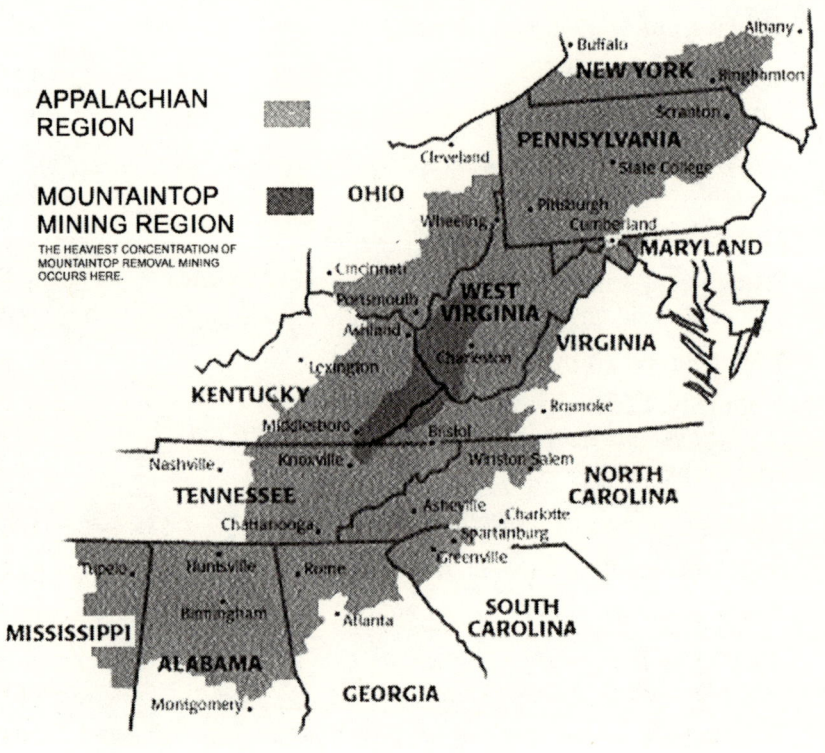

"Appalachia is that somewhat mythical region with no known borders. If such an area exists in terms of geography, such a domain as has shaped the lives and endeavors of men and women from pioneer days to the present and given them an independence and an outlook and a vision such as is often attributed to them, I trust to be understood for imagining the heart of it to be in the hills of Eastern Kentucky where I have lived and feel at home and where I have exercised as much freedom and peace as the world allows."

    James Still, *The Wolfpen Notebooks*.
    Lexington: University Press of Kentucky, 1991.

photo by Kent Kessinger

Appalachian Stream

Foreword

The Human Cancer: Mantra for Survival

by Paul Corbit Brown

Imagine you are on a space station that has been thrown out of orbit. You are now hurtling through space with no outside resources. Your tiny little home has only a limited ability to produce food, oxygen and energy. How would you respond? Would it be fair that the wealthiest member of the crew be allowed to eat as much as (s)he wanted? Would it be fair (or responsible) that this member also was allowed to consume energy without regard for the other members of the station? Would you vote to systematically dismember the station to burn for fuel? Or would a better solution be to assess the realistic capabilities of the station and adjust everyone's consumption accordingly?

Welcome to Planet Earth. We are all passengers on a tiny blue spaceship that has only a finite ability to be *mined*, farmed and burned. This planet is the life support system for all its inhabitants. This includes life forms other than simply humans. The good news is that the earth is a beautiful machine with the very special ability to provide all that we need to survive—if the system is kept in balance. The bad news (for humans) is that this system will ultimately balance itself. If we cannot learn to keep our consumption in check, Nature will remove us from the equation. Cancer is the uncontrolled reproduction and growth of cells in a living organism. Cancer thrives by producing more of itself and consuming its host at a rapid pace. Ultimately, however, it consumes so much that it kills its host and then dies with it—nature always keeps consumption in balance.

Members of industrialized nations have succumbed to an *Entitlement Mentality*. We believe we are entitled to consume all the resources we want. I have often heard people say they feel they have the right to use as much electricity or gasoline as they choose, if they can afford to pay the bill. This is wrong and blatantly irresponsible. Here is the simple truth: *The consumption of energy is no one's right.* It is everyone's responsibility. Basic human rights do not include the right to unbridled consumption of any form of energy or resource—especially that which comes from finite sources.

The true cost of all fossil fuels is not the price we pay at the pump or the power meter. Gas pump and power meter prices don't reflect the cost of environmental degradation. These costs are only now being realized because of global warming, oil spills, war for control of resources, *coal slurry and ash spills*, and adverse effects on the health of individuals who live and work in areas where energy sources are produced.

Renewable energies are perceived as inadequate primarily because of the projections of supply vs. demand. At this point, renewables cannot meet the demand. So how do we solve this? Our first response is to build more power plants, mine more coal, split more atoms and drill for more oil (all for the comfort and ease of the wealthiest passengers on Planet Earth). The better solution is to attack the supply/demand equation from both ends. Rather than simply find ways to produce more energy, we need to find ways to REDUCE our consumption.

Every day we are inundated with complaints that renewable energy is too expensive, not able to meet the demands placed on the grid, etc. ad nauseam. We have misconstrued the notions of *Need* for *Want*. We have come to believe that we need all that we want. Our priorities must be re-evaluated. We do not need to consume with impunity. We *do* need clean energy because we need clean air and clean water. We *do* need to take our role as stewards of this planet seriously.

There are as many solutions to the energy crisis as there are people who consume that energy.

Reduce, Reuse, Recycle—this is our Mantra for Survival.

Introduction

Sacred Responsibility

by Delilah F. O'Haynes

Land has always been important to me and others who grew up in rural America; without the "good earth," one does not eat. I learned early from my grandfather, who farmed the steep hills of Virginia, that land and resources must be preserved, by rotating crops, taking only what one needs, and leaving the strongest plants and animals to reproduce for future use. I learned from my father and mother that the land—the deep forest where I was born and raised—holds everything I need to survive. Respect it, I was taught. Be thankful for it. Leave it as I found it: sacred and whole.

When we flip a light switch, do we think about where the energy for that power comes from? If coal or natural gas was used to produce it, it is very likely that it was obtained through the destruction of mountains and mountain communities. West Virginia has lost enough mountain land to equal the state of Rhode Island, in order to give us power for dishwashers and microwaves. Kentucky has lost similar acreage, and Virginia has lost a third of this acreage. Coming behind coal companies that obtain coal through surface mining are natural gas companies that displace area water supplies and, thereby, families and communities.

Each time a mountaintop is leveled as a cheap way of reaching the coal within that mountain, deadly minerals and chemicals are released into our water and air. In West Virginia alone, three million pounds of ammonium-nitrate and diesel fuel are used each day to make bombs that destroy mountains. By manufacturers' own admissions, ammonium-nitrate must carry a hazardous warning label because it is dangerous if breathed or leached into water sources. Sludge dams which hold the run-off once the coal is washed contain lethal minerals, such as mercury, lead, and arsenic; dozens of these dams in this state are leaking and in danger of breakage. West Virginia's air quality is among the nation's worst, and asthma cases in this state are on the rise.

photo by Delilah O'Haynes

Appalachian Ridge Scene

In the southwest region of Virginia, natural gas wells dot the landscape where families and farm owners are packing up their belongings and placing "For Sale" signs on their properties because their wells, ponds, and creeks have been displaced by these wells. In addition, eroded mountains gawk from horizons where logging companies have clear-cut timber indiscriminately, leaving flooding potential in their wakes.

Why should the rest of America care what happens in West Virginia, Kentucky, Virginia, Tennessee, or other coal-producing states? You should care because toxins from Appalachian mountaintop removal sites poison rivers and streams all the way to the Gulf of Mexico. North Carolina cares about the way their energy is obtained. In May, 2008, North Carolinians introduced the Appalachian Mountains Preservation Act, which would ban the use of coal obtained through the use of mountaintop removal. This ban recognizes that preservation of mountains is not just about preserving beauty or tourism, but it is also about preserving natural resources for our children and obtaining and using resources in responsible ways. While we certainly hope that other Appalachian states will follow this lead, ultimately we need a federal mandate against any environmental practice that would seek to obtain resources for energy at the expense of the welfare of our people and families. According to *Bristol Herald Courier* writer, Debra McCown, Appalachian environmentalists predict the end of mountaintop removal in the near future by just such a mandate. However, we insist that such a mandate demand safer, more environmentally friendly mining and logging practices, if not the end of carbon-based fuel use altogether. We call for the end of big companies coming into Appalachia to plunder her resources at the expense of her people. We demand an end to the destruction of Appalachia.

For those of us who live in the midst of the destruction, we deal with more than a question of resources. We deal with higher cancer rates, higher rates of lung disease, reduced job opportunities, loss of family homesteads, lack of hope for the future, and much more. Coal, natural gas, and logging companies say they provide jobs and keep America running. Those who work for these companies would not dispute that. I, too, understand how the miners and families of miners feel. I'm the daughter of a Virginia coal miner. Coal miners are hard-working people who sacrifice their very bodies to feed and clothe their families. Many people in these mountains have known nothing else for more than a hundred years. Coal mining pays bills and puts food on the table. This has been the stance of the coal miner and logger since mining and logging companies first came to our hills and valleys over a hundred years ago, promising prosperity to the people if they would sell their mineral rights. Those companies didn't want the land, just the timber and coal. Natural gas companies now say the same. The people have been welcome to keep the land. Now the companies take that, too, plus the water supplies. Where does it end?

Logic tells me that once these companies have laid waste our mountains and streams, we will have little on which to build, few resources left to use ourselves, much less to provide jobs and stable communities. Those who haven't seen mountaintop removal—or felt the impact of run-off from clear-cut logging or sunken wells from natural gas lines—might say we can't predict the future. However, if the past is any indicator of what lies ahead, we who have grown up eating and breathing coal dust know all too well what the big companies leave behind once they have taken what they want from a mountain community. If it's indiscriminate logging, stripping, and mountaintop removal, what happened in the Buffalo Creek Disaster in 1972 after a coal company dam collapsed, is an example: 125 people dead, 4000 people left without homes, 16 neighborhoods displaced, according to Mimi Pickering who documented the destruction for *Appalachian Voices.*

People who live near removal and logging sites or natural gas wells would not consider what residents receive in exchange for the removal of resources a fair bargain: destruction of their homelands and homes, toxic air and water, displaced and obliterated wildlife, displaced water supplies, and total annihilation of all resources. But those who depend on out-of-state companies for their survival don't dare say a word against industry practices because they feel they have no recourse, no choice.

But there are choices. With our mountains and rivers and diverse wildlife, we in Appalachia have the potential to create renewable, clean energy sources, such as solar and wind, and to maximize revenue through tourism and outdoor recreation—mountain climbing, hiking, biking, white-water rafting, skiing, four-wheeling, hunting, fishing, and more—all of which provide clean family fun and leave the environment safe for habitation. As soon as agricultural experts know which crops are best to produce "biofuels," according to *National Geographic* writer, Joel K. Bourne, Jr.—such crops as fast-growing trees, perennial grasses, algae—Appalachia can grow them. Our communities were agricultural before coal extraction, and we can be agricultural again—if the land is not destroyed. We would insist, of course, that these renewable resources be harvested in ways that do not harm the communities.

Where alternative industries are concerned, West Virginia has the potential to replicate what Northeast Tennessee and Southwest Virginia are doing with tourism, which is providing those states with thirty billion dollars a year in revenue. According to the *Bristol Herald Courier,* tourists no longer desire beach or theme-park vacations. They want authentic experiences in such places and events as national forests, heritage festivals, vineyards, landmarks, eco-tourist spots, historic districts, natural attractions (such as caves), and the like. Some of the money made in Tennessee and Virginia is made through theme parks and NASCAR, but much of it is made by small business owners who maintain four-wheeling trails, create mazes through their corn fields, and provide cozy getaways in home-town bed & breakfasts. The best thing about small businesses such as these is that the money made stays in the area, benefitting local people seven times over, rather than going out of state to a large coal or gas company. Unfortunately, new natural gas wells coming into southwest Virginia are threatening this thirty-billon-dollar boon.

Renewable energy, responsible use of resources, and jobs that benefit future generations are choices we can make for the sake of our children and grandchildren. We must stand with others and advocate that state governments, as well as our national government, reject the use of mountaintop removal, clear-cut logging, and indiscriminate gas lines in favor of safe, renewable energy and industries that grow local economies. All the voices within this anthology, *Appalachia's Last Stand*, are those of real people in Appalachia who have chosen to speak out in order to save our precious Appalachian resources and heritage. The Appalachian Consortium of Writers involved in this project promised the people in the regions hardest hit by mining, logging, and gas companies that we would make a record of their voices so that they could be heard. We have kept our promise, and in so doing, have made a united stand for the sacred land and people of Appalachia.

If our great-grandfathers could give us advice, they would know that flattened mountains, stripped of topsoil, are useless; little will grow in wasteland. They would show us that trading energy obtained through natural gas for the loss of our water supplies is a foolish endeavor. They would teach us to take mature trees but leave smaller trees for future consumption and for the health of the land. They would remind us that every action we take affects our offspring to seven generations. They would speak traditional wisdom, telling us that one does not "cut off his nose to spite his face." They would teach us the old principles, such as rotating crops to preserve the land, the very source of life-giving food. And they would warn us: make the right choices now, while there is land and clean water left to preserve. Would we listen?

We ask you to hear the voices within this anthology and make a choice to help us stand against the destruction of our homelands. The fight to save our water, our air, our mountains, our heritage and way of life, is truly Appalachia's last stand. To join us in this fight, contact one of the organizations on the following page to find out what you can do to help.

Contacts for Information and Involvement:

Coal River Mountain Watch—www.crmw.net
Kentuckians For The Commonwealth—www.kftc.org
Ohio Valley Environmental Coalition—www.ohvec.org
Save Our Cumberland Mountains—www.socm.org
Southern Appalachian Mountain Stewards —www.samsva.org
West Virginia Highlands Conservancy—www.wvhighlands.org
Appalachian Citizens Law Center—
        www.appalachianlawcenter.org
Appalachian Voices—www.appalachianvoices.org
Appalshop—www.appalshop.org
Heartwood—www.heartwood.org
MACED—www.maced.org
Sierra Club Environmental Justice Program—
        www.sierraclub.org/coal
Southwings—www.southwings.org
Friends of the Mountains—www.friendsofthemountains.org
United Mountain Defense—www.unitedmountaindefense.org
West Virginia Environmental Council—www.wvecouncil.org
Sludge Safety Project—www.sludgesafetyproject.org
I Love Mountains—www.iLoveMountains.org
Stop Mountain Top Removal—www.stopmountaintopremoval.org
Voices For Appalachia—www.voicesforappalachia.org

photo by Paul Corbit Brown

Mountaintop Removal Mining

8

Appalachia's Last Stand

An Open Letter to West Virginia Citizens and the Congress of the United States:

On October 17 and 18 [2006], sixteen writers gathered in the heart of West Virginia to hear testimony and witness first hand the grievous effects of mountaintop removal mining. We learned these five devastating facts:

1. Toxic heavy metals—such as mercury, copper, arsenic, lead, and selenium—have been released into the water system which feeds the Ohio and Mississippi Rivers. This injures not only local residents but threatens water systems all the way to the Gulf.
2. Dozens of dams (built from mining refuse to contain the toxic waste from mining and cleaning coal) are in danger of breaking. One holds over 3 billion (3,000,000,000) gallons of toxic sludge just 400 yards from Marsh Fork Elementary School. This sludge dam holds back *twenty times* as much toxic muck as the one at Buffalo Creek, whose rupture killed 125 people in 1972.
3. Coal companies have decapitated 474 mountains through the Appalachian region. Almost 1,000,000 acres of mountains have been leveled. West Virginia has lost 500,000 acres.
4. Every day in WV, three million (3,000,000) pounds of ammonium-nitrate and diesel fuel are used to blow up mountains. This also releases untold quantities of coal and silica dust into the air.
5. People's homes, property, and businesses have been damaged and destroyed as a direct result of mountaintop removal. In a single 2001 case, 1,500 homes were lost in a flood. The Federal court in Raleigh County, WV, has held the coal, landholding, and timber companies liable for this devastation.

In human terms what does this mean? This is what coal-field natives say:

- This is not a story. These are our lives.
- My children go to bed with their shoes on, so they can run in case of a flood.
- I never imagined I'd sit on my front porch, watching the horizon disappear.
- The first ones going to get it is our little children.
- Where will our kids live, and our grandkids, and our children's grandkids?
- Our golden years have turned to black years.
- We're prisoners in our own homes.
- Greed is overcoming common sense.
- Why should I sell my home, when they are breaking the law? No one should have to live like we are.
- Why destroy our homes for 30 years' worth of energy? Why destroy our land, our air, our water?
- This is not an act of God; this is an act of greed.
- You're bound every where you turn.
- This is not only a coal-field thing; this is a global thing.
- This is a war zone. Not only do we have to fight the companies, but we have to fight our cousins and neighbors.
- A man shouldn't have to poison his neighbors to feed himself.

We do not blame individual miners for struggling to support their families. They, too, are being forced to participate in the demise of their own culture. But this systematic destruction cannot be allowed to continue.

The fight against mountaintop removal will continue in Appalachia, and ultimately the struggle for justice must extend beyond our borders. We call for the end of mountaintop removal, and we call on the United States Congress to take immediate action to save our children, our people, and our mountains.

From writers who live in West Virginia, Virginia, Kentucky, and Ohio:

Bob Henry Baber
Adam Brown
Laura Treacy Bentley
Katie Fallon
Diane Gilliam Fisher
Denise Giardina
Chris Green
Jeff Mann

Sam L. Martin
Irene McKinney
Rob Merritt
Delilah F. O'Haynes
Edwina Pendarvis
Kathy Pleska
John Van Kirk
Beth Wellington

Appalachia's Last Stand

Through these Words and Photographs the Appalachian People Speak

The Obama Administration is investigating mountaintop removal permits. Senator Lamar Alexander has introduced the Appalachian Restoration Act, which strengthens the Clean Water Act by prohibiting the placement of mining wastes into waterways. The EPA is reviewing hundreds of removal permits, and judges have begun to nullify dumping permits. We applaud these efforts to curtail the destruction of Appalachia and save our resources and environment.

However, these endeavors are weak. Ultimately, mountaintop removal must be halted to save Appalachia and help reverse the effects of this environmental scourge. In addition, permanent policies must be put into place to restrict all toxic wastes, regulate the natural gas industry, and restrict logging in order to protect our waterways, air quality, and communities. For the sake of preserving Appalachia and stopping global warming, we demand that these policies be instituted now.

The Appalachian Mountains must not be sacrificed for cheap energy.

photo by Delilah O'Haynes

Appalachian Vista

Buffalo Creek: Two Stories

Tanya Adkins: it was criminal negligence

The rushing waves of black water on a rainy Saturday morning over 30 years ago tore a hole in people's lives that has never been mended. We were visiting an aunt in Ohio when we got the news that the Buffalo Creek dam had burst. I remember the awful drive home, wondering if my aunts, uncles, and cousins on Buffalo Creek were alive or dead. The telephone lines were down, and then Governor Arch Moore had called in the National Guard to close off the area. Unable to get any news, two of my uncles climbed to the ridge tops and walked into Buffalo Creek.

The first thing they encountered was a makeshift morgue where they were asked to identify bodies. The shattered, blackened remains of a man, woman, and child could have been my aunt, uncle, and their daughter. The bodies were so mangled that my uncles couldn't be sure. Fortunately, they later found that all of my family had made it to safety. One hundred and twenty-five others were not as fortunate.

When the National Guard reopened the area, we drove down there. I remember seeing furniture in trees and houses smashed into splinters. I was eight-years-old, and I remember thinking how awful the flood had been. Years later, I realized that it was criminal negligence by the Pittston Coal Company that caused the deaths of all those people.

The coal industry and many state officials have long treated the people of the coalfields as a disposable resource. Speaking after the disaster, Governor Moore said, "The only real sad part is that the state of West Virginia has taken a terrible beating which far overshadowed the beating which the individuals that lost their lives took, and I consider this an even greater tragedy."

This blatant disregard for human life still permeates the political atmosphere of the state. Coal companies are allowed to continue operations, even after repeatedly releasing toxic black sludge into streams and water supplies. Permits are issued to build massive slurry impoundments with the potential for destroying even more lives than were lost on Buffalo Creek. Then, the coal industry works relentlessly to marginalize any dissenting voices.

One of the latest victims of the coal industry's effort to silence the truth is Jack Spadaro. He was a member of the ad hoc commission Governor Moore appointed to investigate the Buffalo Creek disaster. Over the next several years, he worked to improve the safety level of slurry impoundments in the state. Now, Jack Spadaro is in danger of losing his job as the superintendent of the National Mine Safety and Health Academy because he spoke out about federal and industry failures regarding the investigation into the 2000 Martin County coal slurry spill near Inez, KY. (Since this article was written Spadaro has left NMSHA.)

The residents on Buffalo Creek were silenced as well. One woman had written a letter to the governor to complain about the unsafe condition of the dam at least four years before it broke, but nothing was done about it. Will it take another Buffalo Creek disaster before the officials of this state listen to the people who are being affected by coal slurry impoundments?

The lives of the people on Buffalo Creek were valuable, and the lives of those living in harm's way today are valuable. How long will it be before state officials and the Bush administration realize that the lives of people are immensely more valuable than a chunk of coal?

from Geological Survey Circular 667, *West Virginia's Buffalo Creek Flood*

Reconstructed view of the 3 dams above Saunders, 27 February 1972

14

Patty Adkins: It Should Never Have Happened

The tragedy on Buffalo Creek was years in the making. Pittston Coal Company began dumping coal waste on the middle fork of Buffalo Creek in 1957. By 1968, the coal company was dumping more waste another 600 feet upstream. By 1972, a third dam was built that ranged from 45-60 feet in height.

The people of Buffalo Creek were aware that these dams existed, and were afraid that they might break. In 1967, the US Department of the interior warned state officials that the Buffalo Creek dams and 29 others throughout West Virginia were unsafe. Furthermore, Pittston had a record of mining and safety violations. Still, neither the state nor mining officials made any effort to deal with the problem of the slurry impoundment on Buffalo Creek. I was 11 years old when the Buffalo Creek disaster occurred. My family lived on Braeholm Hill and we stood there that morning and watched the devastation unfold. Everything seemed to be happening in slow motion as I watched people in houses and vehicles float by. I remember the sound of the black water breaking the houses apart and seeing animals trying to stay afloat in the raging waters. And after the water went down, I remember seeing two men pull the dead body of a woman from a house that had been lodged against the train trestle. At the time, I thought it was a terrible natural disaster. It was only as an adult that I realized all those deaths were caused by the negligence of the coal industry.

The survivors of the Buffalo Creek disaster have to live with the memories of that day. If state officials had taken heed in 1967 when they were warned of the dangers of these impoundment dams, there wouldn't be an anniversary of this tragedy on February 26. State officials today should not let history repeat itself.

Testimonies of Buffalo Creek

Posted by Appalachian Voices HQ in Feb 2007
reprinted with permission of Appalachian Voices

Betty Tackett: It was a nightmare

    I took my children out of the house, and my husband ran across the railroad track to make sure the neighbors weren't still in bed. He told me to take the children up off of the main road. When I got the kids in the car, we lived in front of the ball park, when I was pulling out of the drive way there was a wall of water 20 feet high coming across the ball park. It took out bridges houses and everything.

    It was a nightmare; you'd see bodies and houses torn apart. You just can't describe it. We had no warning whatsoever; even to get out or anything.

    The man that worked with my husband took my kids to his house. We started walking the next day to get out of there. Me and my husband weren't with our children at that time. I didn't lose none of my family and that was the most important thing. We were given help through the Red Cross. It was hard getting started again.

    The coal company knew they were in the wrong. They were checking on that dam the day before it happened but they still didn't tell anybody to get out of there. They just let it go. It had rained a week before. It wasn't nobody's fault really, I guess it was just God's will, but the coal company knew before time that there was danger, so the people should have been warned. The coal company is more responsible for it than God because they were the ones that built it, they didn't give out any information on it, so I'd put more responsibility on them then I would God. There was 125 people killed in that flood and 52 of them were my neighbors and friends … so I hold the coal company responsible.

from Official Report of the Governor's Ad Hoc Commission of Inquiry – *The Buffalo Creek Flood and Disaster*

Aftermath of the Buffalo Creek Flood and Disaster

Uhle Adkins: The guys said the dam was going to be all right

It rained that whole week and the creek was up real big, on that Friday night we stayed up all night watching that creek. The guys came down earlier and said that dam was going to be all right—it wasn't a problem.

It was 5 'til 8 and that's when the power went off, we went down the road three quarters a mile and a trailer was washed off, floated down. I walked to where my house was at, and I looked at nothing, railroad tracks was twisted like pretzels, I walked back to where I did live and there was nothing.

They said the dam was gonna break and he said I don't believe that, so they went back to bed and him and his two children perished. One of his children was one of the kids that was never found.

One of my friends told me if that dam ever breaks it will take everything out from here to Man, and he was right. There was a lot of force behind it and a lot of water. We didn't get anything from the coal companies, a lot of people sued them but I didn't, I didn't lose my family I just lost my home.

'We heard this terrible noise... the pressure was so forceful that it held all the water together and it moved just like a snake ...

Gertie Moore: crying wolf again

Everybody just thought they were crying wolf again. To tell you the truth, had we been living on the main strip, we would have been gone.

We heard this terrible noise and the power went off. We were on the front porch and coming out of the main holler there was a blue house riding on top of this giant wave, and I didn't know it at the time but the Dillon family was in there.

When we saw what had happened I froze on the front porch and Arlene Johnson said hit the hills and everybody just ran.... The water shot down the road, the pressure was so forceful that it held all the water together and it moved just like a snake, it'd take out one house and skip another house.

[One man] would come in and laugh at them for leaving, he went that morning to get raincoats for the men to work on the hill, and when he left he ran into the water and he shot up Ding's holler and when they found him he was wandering around babbling. You can only imagine that your word would have sent everybody home, and saved them.

Revelations 11:18

by Tonya Adkins

I used to go up on the mountainside
To ease my worried mind
But now that mountaintop is gone
It fell to that big dragline

Chorus:
Then I read my Good Book in Revelations
In the eleventh chapter and the eighteenth verse
What will they say on the judgment morning?
When god destroys those who've destroyed the earth

I've seen the rivers run black as coal
I've seen the timber stripped away
I'm told the love of money is the root of all evil
I see that more clearly every day

Chorus

Now if you come to West Virginia
There's one thing I ask before you go
If you see three crosses on the mountainside
Remember those crucified below

Revelations 11:18 "The nations were angry, and your wrath came, as did the time for the dead to be judged, and to give your bondservants the prophets, their reward, as well as to the saints, and those who fear your name, to the small and the great; and to destroy those who destroy the earth."

A True Story of Bears, Mountains, and a Way of Life

by Dianne Bady

The black bear watched us and we watched back. Then she calmly lumbered off. Larry Gibson told us that just the other day he saw over a dozen bears here on Kayford Mountain.

Larry, whose family owns the surface of this mountain in Raleigh County, WV, said that for the first time, bears are starting to chase people. Larry's extended family comes here regularly to camp and to renew family ties. And now the bear population is beginning to cause some concern.

But the bears don't have much choice in the matter. Their mountain habitats are being massacred, and Kayford Mountain is a refuge for them.

On three sides of Kayford, the former mountains have been blasted and gouged by immense mechanized shovels until there's just a vast wasteland of rubble.

And monster machinery is gearing up to rip out more seams of coal by systematically leveling what-used-to-be-mountains. This isn't "just" mountaintop removal strip mining; it's total annihilation of entire mountains.

It's deliberate destruction of headwater streams, as those former mountains are dumped on top of the waterways in the narrow valleys.

I'd guess that by the time A.T. Massey Coal is finished with this previously beautiful area, the mountains will be valleys, and the former valleys will be huge unstable piles of rock and soil.

I'm horrified by what I'm learning about mountaintop removal/valleyfill strip-mining. On a recent commercial flight from Charleston to Atlanta, I was stunned by the number of blasted-off mountaintops I saw below me.

I wasn't appeased by reading the remarks of Bill Rainey, president of the West Virginia Coal Association, who told the Charleston Gazette that "I'll guarantee you there are a lot of mountaintops that don't have any disturbances."

I'm appalled at a recent "oversight" at an Ashland Coal mountaintop removal job which caused the Coal River to be blackened for miles by thick sludge, and which cost a river guide thousands of dollars of tourist business.

I can't help but feel uneasy when I read that an A.T. Massey subsidiary has just purchased more than 50 million tons of coal, primarily in Wyoming and McDowell counties.

How will this coal be mined? With a strong human work force in underground mines? Or with 20-story-high earth-moving equipment that is so expensive it can't be shut down, but must wreak destruction 24 hours a day, seven days a week?

Some of the folks I recently met at the top of Kayford Mountain emphasized that coal companies have always pushed regular people around in this state.

A lot of people believe that these big companies can't be stopped.

But that's what most people said about the company that planned to build the proposed mammoth pulp mill at Apple Grove. And yet that plan seems to be dying.

It took hundreds of people—regular people—to stop the pulp mill.

It will take thousands of people to stop the destruction of West Virginia's mountains.

It's time to roll up our sleeves.

This Summer's Story: Voices of Those Hurt by Mountaintop Removal Mining

by Shannon Bell

"To be a person is to have a story to tell." —Isak Dinesen

There is nothing more worthwhile in my mind than sitting on a front porch and listening to someone tell his or her story. This summer, I had the pleasure of doing just that—listening to the stories of the courageous individuals in the environmental justice movement who are standing up to the coal industry to hold it accountable.

Their stories have become part of my story—the story I take with me back to Oregon, where I'm in graduate school, to share with the students I teach and the friends with whom I talk.

The coalfields of West Virginia became part of my story back in 1999 when I first came to Cabin Creek in southeastern Kanawha County to work as a service-learning intern at Cabin Creek Health Center.

I moved out to Oregon in 2005 to the University of Oregon. I've spent part of the last two summers volunteering with the environmental justice movement and collecting interviews for what will (hopefully) become a dissertation some day.

My project this summer focused on those individuals who are speaking out against mountaintop removal and other coalfield injustices. This is the story of the community—the family—that has emerged within the environmental justice movement. People talked about the unconditional support and strength they feel from the people they have met through their work. While some people admitted that they have lost some friends due to speaking out against coal, they were quick to tell me that they have made far more friends than they have lost. These quotes speak to that story:

> The friends that I had before, we were friends because we were in the same community, but . . . there's a commonality here [within the movement] that we're doing something that is beyond us, and that has brought us together . . . there is a sense of family and a sense of unity, and a sense of union.

And frankly, these people are neat, I mean, there are my heroes, you k now—Judy Bonds, Larry Gibson, all these people who [do this] with little resources and just a big heart and a big sense of responsibility.
—Bill Price

We've bonded together . . . we're all sisters. We're the sisterhood.—Don't mess with the sisterhood! I guess the only way I can put it, I really didn't realize that there was so many caring people out there. And, what makes it even greater—to see so many young people out there wanting to make something better—you know, it just, I guess like Kathy Mattea said yesterday, the word "overwhelms" . . . I think about that so much. I've met so many friends and everybody's been great to me.
—Donnetta Blankenship

photo by Delilah O'Haynes

Appalachian Church

23

We Are Ready for Clean Energy

Press Release from Citizen Action: Climate Ground Zero, the Ohio Valley Environmental Coalition, Coal River Mountain Watch

Eight more arrests following second wave of citizen protest at toxic coal sludge lake and mountaintop removal site. Massey Energy blasting would endanger community, destroy permanent renewable energy potential

PETTUS, W.Va.—This morning five activists, who had chained themselves to a bulldozer and an excavator, and one videographer were arrested for trespassing at a mountaintop removal site. By afternoon, dozens of local residents, friends and supporters from throughout Appalachia converged at the mine's gate. Eight more citizens were arrested in the afternoon action.

The latest wave of protesters, trained in and committed to nonviolence, delivered a letter to mine company officials. The letter, ultimately intended for Massey Energy CEO Don Blankenship, insists that Massey cease the mountaintop removal operation on Coal River Mountain.

Blasting for part of the operation could begin at any time, very close to a nine-billion-gallon toxic coal waste sludge dam called the Brushy Fork Impoundment. Blasting would occur above underground mines close to the dam and the lake of toxic coal waste it impounds.

Instead of mountaintop removal, residents and their supporters are advocating for a wind farm on the site as a safe alternative for cleaner energy and long-term jobs (www.coalriverwind.org.

"I fear for my friends and all the people living below this coal sludge dam," said Gary Anderson, who lives on the mountain near the site. "Blasting beside the dam, over underground mines, could decimate the valley for miles. The 'experts' said that the Buffalo Creek sludge dam was safe, but it failed. They said that the TVA sludge dam was safe, but it failed. Massey is setting up an even greater catastrophe here."

In 1972, a sludge dam operated by Pittston Coal Company failed and killed 125 people in Buffalo Creek, W.Va.

In 2000, a sludge dam operated by Massey Energy in Martin County, Ky., released approximately 300 million gallons of coal waste that broke through into underground mines. The EPA called that the worst environmental disaster in the Southeast.

Then, in December 2008, a coal ash sludge impoundment operated by the Tennessee Valley Authority (TVA) failed near Harriman, Tenn. That disaster released over one billion gallons of toxic sludge that destroyed three homes, damaged twelve more and covered 300 acres.

The Brushy Fork coal sludge impoundment currently contains seven billion gallons and has a nine-billion-gallon capacity.

Residents have lost faith in their state government and taken their plea nationally.

Climate expert James Hansen, the head of NASA's Goddard Institute for Space Studies, said, "President Obama, please look at Coal River Mountain. Your strongest supporters are counting on you to stop this madness."

"We can't sit by while Massey jeopardizes the lives and homes of thousands of people," said Vernon Haltom of Naoma, W.Va. "Governor Manchin and the West Virginia Department of Environmental Protection have proven that they are unwilling to protect the citizens. What do they expect us to do? Will they wait until we're in body bags to take this threat seriously?"

A 2008 report by the federal Office of Surface Mining revealed serious deficiencies in the WVDEP's regulation of coal waste dams (www.wvgazette.com/News/200901110512?page=1&build=cached).

In November, WVDEP approved a permit revision allowing Massey to begin the mountaintop removal operation. Despite citizens' objections, DEP denied public participation in its decision process.

Anderson added, "We need to stop the madness and stop Massey from blowing up our beautiful mountain. We need to go with the better energy option, and that's a wind farm, which is perfect for Coal River Mountain. We could have a green energy future for the country, starting right here."

Arrested in the morning action were Rory McImoil, Matt Noerpel, James McGuiness, Mike Roselle, Glen Collins and videographer Chad Stevens.

Arrested in the afternoon action were Lorelie Scarbro, Larry Gibson, Charles Nelson, Missy Petty, Mary Wildfire, Vernon Haltom, Allen Johson and Heather Sprouse.

photo by Paul Corbit Brown

Sludge Spill Disaster

Super Fly (Ash)? Super *Bad*.

The Cumberland Park Project — Part 1

by Garrett Bobb

On the surface, the Cumberland Park Project sounds like a good idea for Giles County: Create a new commercial building space to attract businesses and create new jobs while simultaneously disposing of waste and generating funds for the school system. If this project sounds too good to be true, it's because it is.

More than a quarter-million cubic yards of coal ash, also known as Coal Combustion By-product (CCB), Coal Combustion Waste (CCW), or fly ash, is being used as fill material for Cumberland Park, raising up a piece of land that lies within the 100-year flood plain of the New River, next to US-460 in Narrows, Virginia.

In a memo to the Virginia Coal Combustion Products Regulation Technical Review Committee on August 8th of last year, Virginia Tech Professor of Crop and Soil Environmental Science W. Lee Daniels, an expert on CCB disposal, said that it is important to "focus on limiting water migration into and through the ash." If you want to keep something away from water, the flood plain of a river is not a good place to do it.

How dangerous is coal ash? When testifying on June 10th of last year before the U.S. House of Representatives' Subcommittee on Energy and Mineral Resources, Lisa Evans, Project Attorney for Earthjustice said, "As coal is burned, its volume is reduced by two thirds to four fifths, concentrating... chlorine, zinc, copper, arsenic, selenium, mercury, and numerous other dangerously toxic contaminants... These wastes are poisonous and can cause cancer or damage to the nervous systems and other organs, especially in children."

When we consider the toxic content of CCB, the lack of regulation in regards to its disposal boggles the mind. Evans testified, "EPA [Environmental Protection Agency] has regulations governing all aspects of the disposal of household trash in landfills... Yet EPA has no such regulations for the disposal of toxic ash that exceeds *hazardous waste* levels for toxic metals."

photo by Elizabeth Spencer

Coal Ash Dump, Virginia

The coal industry and its supporters routinely circumvent and manipulate existing regulations via so-called "Beneficial Use" clauses written into current environmental law. Exploiting this type of clause, the Giles County Partnership for Excellence, the group who initiated the Cumberland Park project, was able to begin using this poisonous material as fill without any public oversight and without so much as a protective liner to prevent the waste from leaching into soil and groundwater.

The coal companies insist that CCB is a safe fill material. Joe Ryder, Environmental Compliance Officer with American Electric Power whose plant in Glen Lyn, Virginia is the source of the CCB, says that "[CCBs] which are used meet required testing parameters for leaching characteristics and a separation from groundwater is maintained... Despite extensive rains early in the project, no changes in groundwater have occurred and all runoff has drained as expected."

Even though those in charge of the project assure that there is virtually no danger, legitimate concerns on the safety of putting this material so close to the water supply remain. Darlene Cunningham of the Concerned Citizens of Giles County, a group organized to stop the project, is worried. "Worst case scenario would be a catastrophic flood that would just take the whole thing into the river... similar to Harriman, Tennessee," said Cunningham, referring to the massive ash sludge spill that occurred there in December. Everyone would like to avoid such a scenario, but Cunningham says, "The leaching that's going to happen, nobody has denied that it's going to happen, it's just a matter of when and how fast."

What appears initially to be a win-win situation for the citizens of Giles County may prove only to be a win for the power company, and a big loss for anyone and anything unfortunate enough to live downstream.

Though dumping has already begun, the Concerned Citizens are far from admitting defeat. Tune in next issue for part 2: what's being done about it and how you can help.

For additional information:

http://www.concernedgilescitizens.org/
http://citizensforbeneficialchange.org/
http://ecoenthusiast.blogspot.com/

http://www.mountainjustice.org.vt.edu/
http://www.ncnr.org/
http://www.gilescumberlandparkproject.org/

Appalachia has a long history of coal waste disasters. The largest and most recent occurred in Harriman, Tennessee on December 22 of 2008. Early that morning hundreds of millions of gallons of coal ash sludge broke through the earthen dam that was holding it back, contaminating tributaries of the Clinch and Tennessee Rivers, covering hundreds of acres with four to six feet of sludge, and damaging houses and power and gas lines. This is the largest environmental disaster of its kind, spilling a volume of toxic material dozens of times the size of the Exxon Valdez spill. Coal is not clean!

photo courtesy of Tennessee Mountain Defense

TVA Coal Ash Sludge Spill, Tennessee, 2008

Kicking Ash! And Taking Names

The Cumberland Park Project — Part 2

by Garrett Bobb

When some neighbors of the Cumberland Park Project learned of the devastatingly toxic composition of the coal ash slated to be used as "fill material" on the banks of the New River, they knew they didn't want it near their water supply. They formed a group to address the issue: Concerned Citizens of Giles County (CCGC).

It soon became obvious the power company and its associates were not interested in hearing what the people had to say. "We had a public meeting in the fall of '07, invited the public, invited AEP, invited the Partnership [for Excellence], which is the owner of the site, and they did not come... but we did have a good turnout," said Darlene Cunningham, member of the CCGC, in a recent interview.

The CCGC circulated a petition against the Cumberland Park project and contacted local and state officials and legislators of all types for support. "We've gone the gambit," said Cunningham. Due in large part to their efforts, a pair of bills proposed by State Senator John Edwards that would prevent future dumping of un-amended fly ash in flood plains have just passed, having failed to do so last year. A public nuisance complaint was also filed locally. It was heard before a Special Grand Jury but got shot down. "There were five people that signed the complaint and none of them were called for interviews," said Cunningham.

Throughout the project, members of CCGC have been monitoring the site and pursuing every legal option to oppose its continuation. This has resulted in several costly setbacks for the Partnership, including drainage modifications to the site and the addition of deceleration lanes for the ash trucks on US-460.

Though not required by regulations, the Giles County Board of Supervisors asked AEP and the Partnership to put in groundwater testing wells and a liner for the site. The liner was deemed to expensive, but they claim to have put in two such wells, which have so far not shown any dangerous levels of contaminants, though it is likely too soon for them to be expected.

photo by Elizabeth Spencer

Coal Ash Dump, Virginia

The CCGC literally broke new ground when, "on December 4th we actually put in two wells of our own," said Cunningham, thereby becoming the first such group to drill their own water testing wells near a coal ash site. The CCGC hope to produce evidence that the ash will in fact leach heavy metals into the groundwater, gain grounds for further legal action against the project, and even to have the existing ash landfill removed from the flood plain before serious contamination occurs.

The leaching risk does not consider the possibility of damage from a catastrophic flood. At a community meeting sponsored by the CCGC on February 21, attorney John Robertson cited the National Weather Service in saying, "Flooding is the largest cause of weather related deaths in Virginia... there has been an increasing frequency of floods in the last ten years." If the earth embankment that holds the ash were to fail during a flood, the resulting contamination would be devastating. "Don't let anyone tell you this fly ash dump is going to be safe. We've seen what it does to people," said West Virginia mountaintop removal activist and guest speaker Chuck Nelson, referring to the high rates of heavy metal-related disease in areas where fly ash has contaminated the groundwater.

The question arises of what to do with the coal ash? According to Lisa Evans of Earthjustice, citing a U.S. Department of Energy report, "Burning coal produces over 129 million tons *each year* of coal combustion waste in the U.S. This is the equivalent of a train of boxcars stretching from Washington, D.C. to Melbourne, Australia." Certainly it is both desirable and inevitable that we transition to a different source of energy in the future, but right now we are dependent on coal and there is already a humongous amount of ash to cope with.

Henry Liu, retired Civil Engineer and president of the Freight Pipeline company, has developed a new method of producing bricks, called Greenest Brick, using fly ash as the primary constituent. Although the low-calcium eastern coal ash produced here in Appalachia is not ideal for the process, Liu claims, "It is definitely possible to build a profitable Greenest Brick factory in Southwest Virginia.... In Western Europe such as Germany, and in Asia such as China, almost 100% of fly ash is used.... Insufficient government encouragement for beneficial use of fly ash is a main reason for insufficient use of fly ash."

Sequestering the ash away in bricks sounds good, but for now at the very least, "you just need to keep it away from water," says Cunningham. That means getting it out of the flood plain.

For the average Blacksburger who wants to get involved in coal related environmental issues, the group Mountain Justice Blacksburg is a great place to start. "I just can't say enough good things about Mountain Justice," said CCGC member James McGrath, at a February 11 talk on campus. MJB has supported CCGC by donating proceeds from a pie auction hosted last fall, and by hosting talks by members of the CCGC.

Darlene Cunningham suggests writing legislators to demand protection from ash being dumped near waterways. "I really feel like at this point in time that's a great thing to do," she said. Specifically the CCGC would like to see public participation required when coal ash is to be utilized under the beneficial use clauses of the Virginia DEQ. She also said, "Locally we could always use a donation here and there, because we do have a lawyer and we do accumulate some bills." If putting heavy metal-laden coal waste in the flood plain of the New River sounds like a bad idea to you, please take the time to help out these dedicated and hardworking neighbors of ours.

Visit the CCGC at http://www.concernedgilescitizens.org/ for more information or to make a donation via Paypal.

Check out Mountain Justice Blacksburg at http://www.mountainjustice.org.vt.edu/ for the latest information on upcoming events and meeting times and locations.

For more information on Dr. Liu's Greenest Brick, see http://www.greenestbrick.com/

You can learn about a worldwide effort to reduce energy consumption and raise awareness of climate change at http://www.earthhour.org/

You can contact State Senator John Edwards about the issue at

Senator John R. Edwards
Senate of Virginia
P.O. Box 396
Richmond, VA 23218
E-mail – district21@senate.virginia.gov

Conversation – West Virginia – Feb 24, 2008

Participants: Ann Marie Boswell, Patricia Feeney, Ruth Ann Price, Owen Stout, and "Dave"

recorded and transcribed by Delilah F. O'Haynes

Owen: I think one of the major problems is absentee landlords, the people that don't live here. The money is coming from out of state. It's basically greed. They come in and they get as much coal as cheaply and quickly as they possibly can, and they're raping the land while they're doing it. They have no regard for the people that live here or the state. They just come in and slash and cut and burn and dig, and then they leave. And all we're left with is a muddy mess. A polluted mess.

Anne: I think the state should make them pay. I think the state should take the land back.

Dave: I had close to thirty years in underground and surface. I worked in the coal industry all my life, and I know that this coal—if you have to mine it—can be mined through the deep mines. That's what we had all those years, and you would have employed more people. You just wouldn't have made as much money as fast as you would doing it by mountaintop removal. When Arch Minerals are through, they don't give a hoot whether Camp Creek floats to Kanawa City or not. They couldn't care less. They don't hire local people. One time there was an article in the Charleston Gazette: out of 300 people they employed, fifteen of 'em was from Cabin Creek and the other 285 were from out of state. So you're not helping yourself when you do this. I know for a fact that most of that coal can be deep mined. We did it for a hundred years, and the companies made a lot of money. So I just can't see mountaintop removal.

Anne: What do they do with that land when it's flat? When I was up in those hills and saw all that bare land, all I could do was cry. Our children can't even use that land. It is sitting up there barren, and our children are going hungry right now. And our men and young folk can't even work. It's destroying me. I took it to my church, and the pastor said not to let it bother me. I paint pictures, and all my pictures are now barren. You can see it in my oil paintings.

Ruth: My concern is not only the destruction of the land; it is the effect that it's having on the people of the community. The sludge ponds—you can see where they're over-run and they're coming over the mountains and into our streams, and therefore into our drinking water. As for myself, I've had health problems. I live next to where there's acid mine water being drained into the creek, and personally myself, some years ago I was diagnosed with cancer. I was going through cancer treatment, and if you've ever had chemotherapy, you know how smells are intensified. The smell from this creek is just a putrid odor—it's unbearable, especially for me when I went through cancer treatments. So that's when I began to try to find out what is this, what it's doing and everything. For the past seven years, I've concentrated on the health problems in my community, and it's amazing. Just in this little small area where I live, the concentration of cancer is just outrageous, and it's not only cancer. It's all sicknesses. Breathing problems. Dementia. COPD—my husband has it bad. All the way up and down the hollow. I wanted to live, and I fought for my life. There were others in the community that lost their battle with cancer, and it's been our concern (we're not experts but we think) that it does have something to do with our health. I set out to find out what is that in the creek and what are the health problems it's causing. And here I sit seven years later, and I don't know any more now than I did seven years ago. Because we live up a hollow, they overlook us. They want to tear the mountain tops off, get the coal, and they don't care what they're leaving behind or how it affects us. I love the mountains. I really hate to see them come in and destroy them, but I'm losing neighbors, so the health is my concern.

Owen: When I left here and went to Detroit for thirty years and got ready to retire, they sent me to retirement classes. They pulled a map down of the United States, and they showed us which states are retirement friendly as far as taking taxes out of your check and the cost of living. On the map, down through the Kanawa Valley was a big red swath. So I asked the man (he didn't know where I was from) why the Kanawa Valley and West Virginia had that big red swath. He said that "in the industry, it's known as 'Death Valley.' Cancer rates are astronomically high and all bad health problems are very widespread. We don't recommend that anyone go there to retire, much less work." The health problem is not known just here. Someone knows what's going on, and they don't care.

Dave: When I went to the cleaning plant (preparation plant where the coal is washed; they create sludge dams), I was the 36th person hired in November of 1977. A couple of weeks ago my brother passed away—from cancer. He had a seniority list of those we worked with. Eighteen of the thirty-six are dead. The mining industry has to be lax in what they're doing, yet the judges say there's no black lung. They say there's no dust to cause this.

Owen: They pumped 22,000 gallons of sludge an hour—twenty-four hours a day, seven days a week—they pumped this slurry. Millions upon millions of gallons of sludge.

Ruth: We have all these abandoned mines—underground mines that are running everywhere, and when they pump the water into sludge ponds and that water runs underground into these tunnels, it's coming out everywhere from every hole in the mines—it's draining out and it's polluting everywhere.

Owen: There's not a hollow that you can't drive up in and not see the effects of acid mine drainage—big red spots where it's leeching out of the mountain; if it's heavy metals, you'll see what looks like a snow fall on the mountain where aluminum and magnesium and all types of metal that's constantly pouring out of the ground right on the surface. You can see where kids have walked in it, animals have tracked in it.

Ruth: I can tell you about the effects it's had. People drive by our house with their shirts pulled over their noses and mouths—they can't stand the odor. I've had company to pull up to the house and get out and say, "Oh, my god, is that your sewer?" And I say, "No, that's the creek." You can go on Google Earth and look down on the creek that runs behind my home. You can see it. It leaves a white trail.

Anne: At some creeks, you've got the pipe coming right out of the ground. Some don't even block them up.

Dave: Those are mines that are on fire. Where you see a vapor or smoke and it stinks, those are from mines that are on fire. We have a lot of those in this state, and it does cause some of the forest fires.

Anne: I'm from Maine, and I've never seen anything like this. When you go into the woods and see dead animals just lying there, it's emotional, you know. This is all new to me. I have pictures where there are deer dead—not just buried or covered up—just dead there. But they died because of the environment. When I found out, I cried. And you're not allowed to say anything. You're not allowed to do anything. They take your land. They take your coal. What you people went through in this state, your state should be made of gold. Your people should have everything they need—health care, everything. West Virginia fought for their coal, the way they had to survive. I'm ashamed of what my mother-in-law had to go through. She and her husband both died—couldn't breathe.

Ruth: They don't even allow you to go there. They have guards. You're not allowed on the property.

Anne: I can't believe they won't build something, put something back on the land. They're always saying they want another permit to take more land. All you do is see more trucks coming out of there, taking more coal. And the dust on the houses. And the accidents. One time I took pictures of coal truck accidents on that road. In one month I think I took pictures of about thirty coal truck accidents.

Owen: We have some places on Cabin Creek where they've reclaimed the mountain. It's a beautiful place, beautiful animal refuge area. But when they get through with their permit, all these beautiful ponds and all these streams, they have to cover them over. They can't leave one inch of standing water. They have to destroy everything because the people that actually own the land are liable. So if you have a beautiful pond back there that's been reclaimed, the land owners don't want the liability of a kid going back there and drowning or getting hurt in one of these areas. These places are show and tell. They can bring a bus load of kids in from Charleston, and they'll take them back there on a bus tour and say, "Look what a beautiful place we've created."

But they'll tell you that the day their contract's over, they'll tear all that out. You won't have access to it. It's all a publicity stunt, basically. Land companies lease out the land for the timber rights, mineral rights, gas rights. A lot of people won't say anything against the coal companies because they live on coal company land. If they say anything negative, they could be gone. In 1996, right above my house (I own my land—I'm one of the few), 17 people were given 30 days to be out. They left and threw a match into the house, and they were gone. They're at the mercy of the coal company and the land owners.

Ruth: In my community, most of the land is owned by coal companies.

photo by Vivian Stockman

Sludge or Slurry Pond

Owen: They had an sludge pond to break up at the head of the hollow, and it put two foot of sludge and muck in these people's yards. And they actually bragged on the coal company—that they did such a wonderful job cleaning it up. They had to say that. If they said anything else, they wouldn't have any place else to go. That's been about four years ago. They'll come in and clean it up lickity-split.

Ruth: If it's where people can see it. If it's up a hollow where there's no community, they don't clean it up.

Owen: Timbering is unrestricted. I went through Vietnam and I didn't see anything like what I saw on the hill right behind my house. It was absolutely utter devastation. They just came in and took timber willy-nilly. They did more damage than MTR. There's areas at the head of the hollow that looks like a moonscape. It has the most god-awful looking muck. It's orange and you can't even walk on it—just as far as you can see. It's oozing hydraulics where they used to "gob." They would pour it in these valleys and fill it up and just the water pressure over the years is forcing it out.

Dave: The bad part is that we have laws but they're not being enforced. This coal could be mined. No one monitors the people. What did they do over in Kanawa State Forest? They went over there to set a gas well and cut a bunch of the forest down. Are we not trying to protect the environment, or do we just not care? I know for a fact that they're not enforcing the laws on mining and timbering.

Ruth: It's not so much that they don't care about the people and the environment. They just want the money.

Owen: It's just like with oil—40 million dollar profit. That's the main force behind it all.

Anne: We could make better profit doing something else—tourism. I mean, you look at the Smokey Mountains. People travel across country to see those beautiful mountains. And we had the same thing here. They could have used that (MTR site) for a race track. They could have had cross-country racing. Instead, I see families in that hollow using drugs. People say, "We want to clean up our area, but we don't know what to do." They could be doing something with this Coal Fork land. There'd be a better chance for the people. But there's no chance because no one takes interest, not even our government in West Virginia.

Ruth: Aren't the coal mining companies supposed to give back to the communities when they take this land so that you can use it in the future?

Anne: Every time you bring something up, they say, "Don't talk about nothing."

Owen: People think West Virginia is like it used to be because in 99% of books, that's what it is. You don't see it publicized the way it is now. What West Virginia used to be is gone—banjo and mandolin playing, people having a good time on their back porch. It's not like that anymore, but they're still projecting that image. I think it should be projected—this is what they're doing to West Virginia. Now you'll get black lung sitting on your back porch. There's two trains that go by my house every day—100-ton coal cars, 150 cars on a train. Twice a day and more than that in coal trucks leaving right by my house. And we've got nothing to show for it but cancer and coal dirt.

Dave: We don't even have guard rails or street lights.

Ruth: We live up these hollows, and they come strip our land, and because we live in the hollow, we're treated as if we live in a third-world country.

Owen: The state looks the other way because they get revenue—from each ton of coal sold, the states gets so much money.

Dave: I don't think the laws are being enforced. If you notice in the last few years where you have these coal trucks that are going through now, they're creating a lot of dust and a lot of people start to get concerned. But all these years it was okay for us to breathe it. I've lived up here all my life, and with this MTR, the way I think a lot of people in this state look at it, if it's in your backyard, it's okay, but don't come to my backyard. We had the thing out here where the people found out they were going to have to look at a strip job. They were jumping up and down.

Owen: I think the coal company used that against us because they know the people in West Virginia are tribal, very tribal. I mean, they try to start little fires and have different people at one another's throat while they go behind our back and tear the mountains down and do whatever they're gonna do.

Dave: But don't do it in my backyard. Do it in somebody else's.

Ruth: You know where they have the tipple, where the tracks come in and out? I went through there the other night and lost the lines. You couldn't see the road because of the coal dirt covering up the lines. My daughter said, "You're on the wrong side of the road." I couldn't tell.

Owen: The creek is like that now. It's got so bad it's like a slurry in the middle of the road.

Dave: And no one's making them take the street sweepers and clean it up. It's getting worse by the day. No one's enforcing the laws.

Owen: I think people are getting disenchanted because they've seen it go on so long and nothing actually happens. I'll give you an example. Right where I live, there's a coal mine, a deep mine, and they're supposed to stop digging when they get to an old abandoned gas well. They can't cut through it because of the danger of explosion or fire. They get to these two gas wells and they say, "Well, what is the fine for cutting through those?" It's $10,000. So they say, "Cut it." They cut it and keep on digging. How much that fine got to be when it got down to Charleston, nobody knows. We hear stories that by the time it gets to Charleston, it's $10. Cutting that gas line is a safety hazard for the miners working around it.

Dave: If you hit the casing on that gas well, you've got major problems.

Owen: You've got potential for an explosion. I can tell you places where they've gone through a graveyard instead of going around or moving graves. A cousin of mine called me and said they were core drilling in an old cemetery where his relatives were buried. They just go in and core drill right down through the graves and then cover it up. So what if it's a fine. Who cares? They don't have any conscience. Their job is to dig coal, and that's what they do.

Dave: If you don't enforce the laws, there's no use making them. The laws are not being enforced right now. And why? Politics.

Anne: Yeah, politics. It is all politics. No one has a conscience.

Owen: I read that Massey said that if you have coal trucks, someone is gonna die. It's almost got to the point now with this MTR that if people don't take back over the stand for the people, someone's gonna die.

Anne: You have to start with the young ones because the older ones don't care.

Dave: Cabin Creek is filling up right now. Now it doesn't take near the amount of rain to widen that creek in a short period of time. There has to be a solution. You can't keep putting this dirt in the bottom of the creek.

Anne: Yeah, sooner or later, you won't have a creek.

Dave: The politicians and officials listen, but they don't do anything.

Owen: It's got to the point in West Virginia that if it doesn't come from the federal level, it's not going to happen. West Virginia is bought and paid for. We are sold to the highest bidder. I think the coal companies think the best thing that could happen to them is if we just left.

Ruth: Where would we go? Myself, because of the cancer, because of the treatments, it left me disabled. Now I live on a limited income. Where am I gonna go that I could live on $650 a month?

Anne: I'm in the same boat. My husband has COPD. I can only work part time because I have to take care of him.

Owen: People are leery of groups coming in. The Army Corp of Engineers came to our watershed meeting, and they were supposed to start digging the next week. We haven't seen them since. Coal companies are supposed to put so much money back into the community, but I haven't seen it. The majority of coal severance tax is supposed to go back into the area where the coal came from, but that's interpreted as Charleston. There's no playgrounds on Cabin Creek. Over 5,000 people and we don't have one playground. No grocery stores. Nothing for kids to do. When I was a kid, there was 15,000 people on Cabin Creek. We had tennis courts, playgrounds, theatres, skating rinks, 30 baseball teams—when coal bottomed out in the 50s. It's all gone.

Ruth: Now you have the coal companies protesting Krogers because Krogers is supporting OVEC.

Owen: I think the coal company pits citizens against OVEC. They don't want anyone who's gonna come in and give them any grief. They want to come and dig what they want to dig and they don't want anyone to say anything.

Ruth: They had the media covering the coal company protesting Krogers, and I said, if you want to see something, let the media go and look at these places they've stripped that looks like you're on another planet. They don't show that.

Anne: My goal is to leave something to the younger generation. It's about time.

Dave: I don't feel that the politicians have our interests at heart at all. It's money, money, money. You have to be a billionaire to do anything in politics, and if you've got the money, you can do what you want and get away with it. Look what Blankenship has done. He has absolutely tried his best to ruin this state. I'm retired from the union, and I shouldn't say what I say, but it just burns me up. They're gonna let Massey ruin this state.

Ruth: Blankenship and Massey want to ruin West Virginia.

Dave: I know people have to work and make a living, and I even tell people that, but boy, when they get ready to retire, boy are they gonna be in trouble. I'd get repercussions for saying that, so just call me "Dave." Everybody knows what politics have done. We all know what's going on. If they don't get this retirement straightened out soon, what are they gonna do? These greedy people got in office and couldn't do the job and made bad investments, but they had money to get in office. I think we're going in the wrong direction. Wyoming (County) has strip mines that are unreal. They make ours look like a playground. The reclamation when they get through, you cannot tell that there was even an ounce of coal mined. If they can do it, why can't we do it? As they go down and get the coal, they start backfilling. As they move the coal out, they fill it back in. Then they start planting grass and trees. You can't tell there was ever a mine there. Now, it's flat land. But if they've got that good a reclamation, why can't we have just a little reclamation?

Delilah: It shouldn't be called mountaintop removal. It's mountain removal. Can you reclaim it? You've totally torn the mountain down, and you've thrown up all that mercury and lead and arsenic that's underneath. And then you've dumped all that stuff in the valleys. Where is your top soil? Your top soil is gone. How do you reclaim it? Could you reclaim it?

Dave: I don't know how you could reclaim it. I'm not sure that you could reclaim it. But there are other ways of mining it. You don't have to move that mountaintop. There are all kinds of different types of mining now. The reason: GREED. You can make more money with MTR than you can deep mining.

Owen: It's the demand for coal.

Patricia: I'm interested in your ideas of solutions—what you all have tried and what you've seen people try. At what point did you become willing to speak up?

Ruth: The way you get more people to speak up is by educating them.

Dave: Yeah. They don't have a clue. Unless you see it, you don't have a clue.

Owen: I think it's too late. West Virginia is bought and paid for. Unless you could get federal judges to come in. You could take till the cows come in. We're sold.

Anne: And when you go to the Capital and talk to the House of Representatives, they look at you like you're an idiot.

Owen: If they stopped MTR today, we would never clean this state up.

Ruth: Seven years ago I was ignorant too. I didn't know what a sludge pond had to do with anything. I do believe if people understood what we're trying to accomplish, I believe more people would stand up.

Dave: People have the attitude of, "Well, it doesn't affect me, so why should I care?" But it DOES affect them.

Patricia: Do you think people have any sense of the national legislation and how people are organizing around the country?

Owen: I think people are so caught up in trying to survive day to day—with the disease and the poverty. 89% of our school kids qualify for free lunches. So people are more tied up in just trying to survive day to day than trying to tackle an issue as big as MTR.

Ruth: The coal companies say that without them here mining the coal, we wouldn't have a job.

Owen: And they're right. That's all there is in West Virginia—coal and chemicals. People know if they go out and fight, their sons or their daughters or their aunts or their uncles will lose their jobs. That's all there is—coal and timber.

Ruth: I'm just one person fighting a losing battle (tainted water). We've tried to form groups, but people get so disgusted that they get nothing done. It's like, why bother?

Owen: How they got around testing the water on Cabin Creek is that we got city water.

Patricia: We need to do a better job of getting resources at the community level. We want to get big issues out to the media, but in the meantime we have people fighting real-life battles. So if you all have any ideas or suggestions about resources and connections or about ways we can fill gaps.

Owen: I think we stay so broad that nobody sees anything accomplished. There's no enforcement of any laws. With the mining industry, it's so blatant that it's a joke. Coal trucks come out of cabin creek with double the amount they're allowed to have. Nobody cares. When I was a kid, the work ethic on Cabin Creek was phenomenal. But anymore, nothing, zero.

Dave: When we grew up—fifty years ago—we had one of the best coal companies in the world.

Owen: We had top notch schools, medical, everything. GREED.

Dave: Yeah, at Christmas they gave their workers gifts and fruit and turkeys. That's when they cared about their people. Family values meant a lot to 'em. Now, money is the name of the game. Now Massey makes a lot of their employers sign a contract. You'll make big money. A friend of mine was told if he didn't sign the contract, he wouldn't go to $24 an hour. That contract says you'll go where they tell you and you have to stay for two years. If you quit, you have to start paying the money back. Politics. Money.

Anne: I hope they do something with the barren land.

Ruth: I have an uncle dying from lung cancer right now. They're saying it's because he smoked. The only way you can prove you've got black lung is to die and have an autopsy done.

Dave: In the 1970s, when we all went for black lung tests, they gave everybody 5%. Then twenty years later, they say we don't have black lung after being in the mines thirty years.

Anne: I hope we can leave something to the children.

My Neighbor has a TV in His Garage

by Dave Cooper, July 2007

In February I found myself in a huge snowstorm as I drove into Cincinnati. Suddenly the interstates stopped moving, all the main roads and even some of the back ways through Cincinnati became gridlocked as the snow came down. Schools closed early and businesses sent all their employees home—which further clogged the roads. Unable to go north to my destination (Detroit), and unable to return to Lexington, I decided to pass the day by visiting some old friends in my hometown of Wyoming, Ohio. These friends lived on the same street I lived on when I was in middle school. They had three little girls, and school was out, so we decided to spend the afternoon sled-riding.

We went to the top of the street, to the backyard of a house which was famous for sled-riding, at least among the local kids. The house looked sad and vacant and a little bit neglected, so I asked what had happened. My Ohio friends informed me that the owners had been very ill and the children didn't want to sell the house, so it had just been left sitting vacant for a number of years.

Then I noticed the smoke rising from the chimney.

They still had the heat turned on—in a house that had been vacant for years.

I get really frustrated when I hear politicians and bureaucrats claim that we have to build all these new power plants, and turn coal into liquid oil, and drill in the Arctic National Wildlife Refuge to meet America's rising energy demands—as if there was some cosmic, immutable law that says America's consumption of our natural resources must always increase, forever. America already uses over 25 percent of the earth's natural resources, even though we only have five percent of the world's population. We are blowing up the mountains for coal, and plundering the oceans, and now we are even talking about strip mining the northern half of the Canadian Province of Alberta to get to the tar sands underneath the boreal forest.

It's madness, and there is no end in sight.

Almost no one in the leadership of this country is talking about energy conservation, but there is so much waste, so much unnecessary usage of electricity and natural resources.

I wonder how many vacant houses there are in America with the heat or air conditioning turned on right now? I wonder how many homes have the television blaring into an empty room right now. I wonder how many schools and office buildings leave their computers turned on all night long.

My neighbor has a television set—in his garage. I've been to UK college football games with all the floodlights turned on—at 1:00 in the afternoon. A good friend of mine insists on leaving house lights on for the cat, so they won't be left in the dark. And many of the old college buildings I visit on my speaking tour are so over-heated that people open the windows in the middle of winter just to cool off.

That's the way we use energy in this country. We are the generation of Americans that will use up all the coal, all the natural gas, all the minerals and all the oil so that we can watch television in the bedroom and drive Hummers to the shopping mall. And we are leaving nothing for the next generation of people who will be on this planet except flattened mountains and landfills bulging with plastic wrappers and aluminum cans, because we as a society were just too stupid, too selfish and too lazy to conserve.

Lately I've been thinking that a smart operator should begin buying up the mineral rights to the municipal landfills in this country. We already see landfill scavenging in third world countries like the Philippines. How long until it becomes profitable to start digging up trash mountains in America to recover bits of formerly plentiful metals like copper and aluminum?

I wonder what people a hundred years from now are going to think about us. Will they curse us? Will they call us "the evil ones?" Will we be called the stupidest generation in all of human history?

Yes, I know that guilt is not a good way to motivate people. And for those of you with televisions in your bathroom, I'm sorry for ranting. I just get tired of hearing people complain about high taxes, high gas prices, or the high price of utilities, when so many people are doing almost nothing to try and use less energy.

At our house, we've cut our utility bills way down by using compact fluorescent bulbs, an Energy Star refrigerator, a new high-efficiency furnace and using a low flow toilet and showerhead. The typical home in the Southeast uses 1,100 KW-hrs of electricity each month. Our houses uses between 250 and 300 KW-hrs each month, but we haven't diminished our quality of life at all. And best of all we save money every month on our utility bills—less profit for the corporate polluters like Kentucky Utilities and E.On, and more money in our pockets.

To learn more about energy conservation in the home, go to www.kilowattours.org and order a copy of their excellent documentary film.

photo courtesy of Kentuckians For The Commonwelth

Mountaintop Mining in Kentucky

Climate Change Denial

by Dave Cooper, June 2008

When I first graduated from college with a Mechanical Engineering degree, I went to work for a General Motors auto assembly plant in Norwood, Ohio, just north of Cincinnati. We made Camaros and Firebirds, but the Detroit GM bosses were unhappy with our productivity, labor relations and quality standards. They constantly threatened us with dire consequences if the plant didn't improve.

It seemed unthinkable that such a massive plant operated by the largest industrial powerhouse on the planet, General Motors—with two shifts producing one of the hottest muscle cars in America—would ever shut its doors. I remember hearing the guys on the factory floor laughing about it. "They'll never close this plant down!"

And of course they did, and 6,000 good-paying union jobs were lost forever.

In my senior year of college (1980), I went to New Orleans for spring break, and I learned that the city was actually below sea level, that storm water had to be pumped up hill into the Mississippi River, and that massive earthen levees held the river back and prevented flooding. "If we ever had a bad enough flood, this whole city would be under water," my college buddy Delmar Caldwell told me. Well—that'll never happen, I remember thinking. A city the size of New Orleans, under water? Impossible.

And then there is the tragic story of the Buffalo Creek flood in 1972, where a coal refuse dam in West Virginia suddenly failed and unleashed a wall of water into a crowded hollow, killing 125 people and destroying 4,000 homes. During the investigation of the disaster, government officials questioned the Pittston Coal mine engineer responsible for the dam, Steve Dasovich, about why the dam had been so poorly constructed and designed.

In testimony before the US Senate three months after the disaster, Mr. Dasovich stated, "as massive as that structure [dam] was, failure was the furthest thing from my mind. To conceive of a mass that large which was close to a million tons of material … was beyond my conception of being possible to fail."

photo by Vivian Stockman

Kayford Mountain, West Virginia

And that is the way the human mind works. If something is so terrible that we cannot even imagine it, then it cannot happen.

How many times must we humans learn that bad things happen, even though we don't want them to?

When we see the slides of Al Gore in "An Inconvenient Truth" showing possible inundation of Florida, Manhattan, and San Francisco caused by Greenland's ice melting, our minds reel. It can't actually happen, can it?

In his 2005 essay "The Ends of the World as We Know Them," Pulitzer Prize-winning author Jared Diamond ("Collapse", "Guns, Germs and Steel") says that "History warns us that when once-powerful societies collapse, they tend to do so quickly and unexpectedly ... a major factor [in the collapse of Mayan civilization] was environmental degradation by people: deforestation, soil erosion and water management problems."

Well, thank goodness we don't have those kind of problems in America today!

Are we Americans all living in complete denial? Do we think that if we don't want climate change to happen badly enough, if we wish and wish, then it won't happen?

I don't like to fixate on this troublesome subject. It's depressing as hell.

But one person who does is Derrick Jensen, the author of "Endgame." In his Ten Principles which preface the book, Jensen proposes that the sooner industrial civilization collapses, the better it will be—for those who are left. In other words, if civilization takes another 500 years to descend into anarchy or oblivion, it will be much worse than if it happens now, because 500 years of population increases means more people will suffer.

Also, there will still be some natural resources left if civilization falls apart next week, and those resources might actually sustain the "Mad Max" and "Waterworld" type scavengers who survive the crash. If you have the stomach, you can watch a two hour lecture by Jensen on Google Video (just search "Derrick Jensen.")

I find Jensen's message appalling and somewhat dangerous. Timothy McVeigh was inspired by a book like this called "The Turner Diaries." There are unstable people everywhere, and what happens if some nut with access to smallpox germs or nerve gas actually takes Jensen's message to heart?

And yet I have friends that I respect who believe that Jensen's ideas are worthy of consideration and discussion.

I've got a better idea. Instead of figuring out the best way to survive the end times, let's save the planet instead.

Appalachian Regional Reforestation Initiative

by Dave Cooper

originally published in the *Tennessee Mountain Defender*

One of the major citizen complaints about mountaintop removal has always been the way that coal companies reclaim the mountains after mining is complete.

Of course, no human driving a D-9 bulldozer can ever recreate the beauty of God's creation. But when ABC's "Nightline" interviewed workers on a mountaintop removal site in West Virginia for its 1998 story "Digging Deep: The Cost of Cheap Energy," one operator stated "We're not destroying the land, we're making the land better."

Sadly, the standard coal industry reclamation practice for too many years has been hydro-seeding the barren land with *sericea lespedeza*, an invasive, incredibly prolific plant that is cheap, hardy, and will grow on the side of a telephone pole. Most importantly to the coal industry, it makes the reclaimed land look green when politicians or people like Department of Interior Secretary Gail Norton fly over the coalfields. Now we see lespedeza spreading up and down the highways of eastern Kentucky, invading fields and displacing our native plants.

What's missing from reclaimed mine sites is trees. Despite the claims of Bill Caylor of the Kentucky Coal Association, trees do not grow well on reclaimed mountaintop removal sites, primarily because the hard, compacted land greatly inhibits the growth of tree roots.

Tree roots need oxygen, and coal companies have always compacted the crushed rock on reclamation sites by driving huge bulldozers and heavy machinery across the land. This compaction practice developed after landslides became one of the major coalfield citizen complaints in the 1960's and 1970's. On many reclaimed MTR sites, the soil is as hard as concrete. You would almost need a jackhammer to plant a tree.

Research begun many years ago and currently continuing at the University of Kentucky under the leadership of Dr. Don Graves is offering promise in developing ways that trees can begin to grow on reclamation sites. It's called the Appalachian Regional Reforestation Initiative (ARRI), and you are going to be hearing a lot more about this.

After hearing his presentation on ARRI at a conference in Charleston, in December I joined Patrick Angel of the federal Office of Surface Mining (OSM) for a tour of UK's test plot on the Starfire Mine in Perry County. Mr. Angel, a former surface mine inspector for many years who proudly claims to have written the first Cessation Order under the federal law to a coal company in the 1970's, is now a doctoral Forestry student at the University of Kentucky and the OSM's Regional Forester and Soil Scientist.

On the Starfire site, we first visited a test plot where hundreds of tree seedlings had been planted in 1996 in the compacted soil typically found on a reclamation site. Only a few trees had survived, and others showed signs of stress and disease. Interestingly, the test plot was surrounded by a ten-foot tall electric fence, to keep the Starfire elk from eating the seedlings. Apparently, elk damage is becoming a major nuisance in eastern Kentucky.

Next we visited a second test plot where the mining "spoil" or "overburden" had been dumped in loose piles approximately 10 feet high in 1997, and then gently graded. No topsoil or organic matter had been added to the spoil piles. Many trees were 10 to 20 feet tall, including hardwoods like white oak, black walnut and white ash. Yellow poplar and white pines grew extremely fast on the test site, and the Pawlonia trees (an extremely fast-growing Asian import that is considered by many environmentalists to be an invasive pest) were almost 30 feet tall.

Mr. Angel stated that the loose piles of overburden had been shown to decrease the amount of rainwater runoff from surface mines—an important consideration for flood-prone communities beneath MTR sites—as well as reducing the amount of sediment carried in the runoff. He stressed that the loose spoil dumping method would only be used on the flat tops of mountains—never on the sides or on steep slopes of mountains.

Next we visited a third test site where spoil had been recently dumped and seedlings planted two years ago. It wasn't pretty to look at, and walking across the rough piles was impossible. However, as the trees grow, Mr. Angel assured me that the spoil piles "melt down" and gradually flatten out to look like the second test plot. Planned access roads every 400 feet would allow logging equipment to extract trees without further compaction of the land.

The ARRI is making a lot of waves, and the evident success of the project at growing trees on reclamation sites presents an interesting conundrum for Kentucky environmentalists. Of course we all want to see trees growing on reclamation sites. But growing trees is not the same thing as a healthy forest—what about the understory plants like ginseng and black cohosh? Also, what if the coal industry uses the project as an excuse to keep flattening mountains?

And what about old mine sites abandoned before the SMCRA law passed in 1977? The Abandoned Mine Land (AML) money is supposed to be used to reclaim these lands. Experiments are ongoing to find ways to cut trenches in old mine sites to loosen the soil for tree planting. But will the AML monies ever be released for such a project?

And most importantly: what do the coal companies think about the loose spoil dumping process for reclamation? Will they buy into this plan, and when will they stop creating useless, barren grasslands?

All these questions will play out over the next few years, and it's important for Kentuckians involved in the mountaintop removal issue to learn more about the ARRI. This project has a lot of potential to help solve some flooding and reclamation issues, and establish future logging jobs in eastern Kentucky, or it can be used to greenwash mountaintop removal. It's up to us to get involved.

Sago

by Tom Donlon

"Please, Doctor, I feel a pain.
Not here. No, not here. Even I don't know."
　—Czeslaw Milosz, from "I Sleep A Lot"

They never asked to be born here,
but, in this rolling country, coal runs
deep in their veins. Like their fathers
and their fathers' fathers, they grip
their wife-packed lunches and go
to the mines, or they turn their backs
on king coal and seek the exotic,
the far away. Each has cut his groove,
has found the poison he must drink
to survive. Down into the deep womb
of their beginnings they go, dust to dust,
their black faces glistening in lamplight
as shadows against the dark face of coal—
their wives, anguished, asking why,
when a man, at night, spits up blood,
he goes back down that dank hole.
And we, unknowing, on the outside, rich
in mountain air, see into that gaseous,
cold space, into the dark face of our future.
We will wait for you. Come, tell us
what you found on the other side, whether
one day our faces, like yours, will shine.

used with permission of *Blue Collar Review*

Morning Glories

by Katie Fallon

    The wild morning glories have finally spilled the top two stones from the wall along my driveway. I'd been watching them all spring, the slow, deliberate way their woody trunks thickened. They pushed a little more and a little harder until one summer day, after their purple blossoms unpuckered, a final nudge sent the stones clattering to the pavement. As if to say, I root here. Shove off.

    I watch the morning glory drama from my porch. The birds around me are hard at work, too. I hear the whirring of loud wings as a nuthatch swoops in to hang upside down from a feeder, then flits away to a red oak and begins to hunt for insects wedged under shards of bark. Somewhere a fox squirrel crashes across a branch. Goldfinches argue in the forsythia; I wish I spoke better bird. A mourning dove trills the end of a coo and another answers. Cardinals claim each other while a downy woodpecker hammers a trunk. Field sparrows in the orchard flute down the scale and tufted titmice scold me from the chestnut tree. It's loud out here, so loud that the backdrop almost goes unnoticed—a few ridges over, the smokestacks of Allegheny Energy's plant at Fort Martin puff poison clouds skyward, darkening the blue like dirty cumuli.

    Seven coal-fired power plants operate within thirty miles of this porch, these morning glories, the busy birds. According to the West Virginia Department of Environmental Protection, the Fort Martin plant sends arsenic, formaldehyde, mercury, and other chemicals into the air we breathe twenty-four hours a day, seven days a week. Mercury balls itself up in livers and kidneys, seeps out in saliva and sweat, causes arms and legs to tremor like twigs in a wind storm. What would it do to a chickadee?

    An energy company from Massachusetts is seeking permission to build another power plant one mile from the existing plant at Fort Martin. From my porch I will be able to see smoke and steam from not one, but two coal-fired plants. The new plant's stack will stand 550-feet high, and will be the tallest manmade structure in West Virginia. Rumor has it, the power generated will be sent up north to New England. But as the company's website points out, "Regardless of where the power goes, some 1200 construction jobs, 50 to 60 operations jobs and support industries jobs stay in the region."

Of course they will. This is what we do in West Virginia: we labor. We mine, we construct, and we operate dangerous machinery. We give out-of-state companies tax breaks to flush chemicals into our rivers, belch poison into our skies, and toss us miserable jobs. We have one of the highest childhood asthma rates in the nation. Our economy ranks dead last. And at the end of the day, we thank the coal industry for "making West Virginia great."

I take my lesson from the wild morning glories and write a letter protesting the proposed plant to the West Virginia Public Service Commission. I compose it here, on my porch, in the shadow of a white pine and a smoke stack. A gang of blue jays cheers me on from the oak trees, chanting, *Thief! Thief!* I end the letter, "Thank you for your time," but what I mean is, I root here. Shove off.

photo courtesy of Tennessee Mountain Defense

TVA Coal Ash Sludge Spill, Tennessee, 2008,
Power Plants in the Background

Weapons

by Katie Fallon

I stand at the wooded edge of Larry Gibson's last fifty acres—all that remains of his family's 500—and look down into the vast hole that used to be Kayford Mountain. Far below, massive earth-moving machines rumble across the barren, grayish-brown expanse. The area looks like a freakish amphitheatre roughly carved by a colossal ice cream scooper. Behind me, vibrant red maples quiver in the October breeze. Tiny white asters bravely grow close to the rocky edge, their roots clinging to earth that, in a few months, will probably be gone. I hear a small flock of cedar waxwings in the trees behind me; they fly beyond the treetops, into the empty air above the hole, and seeming shocked, quickly turn and head back for the tree line. I know how they feel.

This mountain, like many others in West Virginia, had the unfortunate geological luck of holding coal below its surface. Once a mountain suitable for mining is identified, an interested coal company finds a way to secure mineral rights. Often, poor and sometimes illiterate landowners generations earlier had sold rights to the minerals, creating a situation in which the current owners of the land might not have a say in the re-sale of what lies *beneath* their land. Mineral rights law is confusing, but as I understand it, the owner of the minerals is legally permitted to extract them by any method necessary. The method being used here on Kayford Mountain, and throughout much of central Appalachia, is known as mountaintop removal. The term "mountaintop removal" is far too gentle; it reminds me of "unwanted hair removal" or "wart removal." In this kind of mining, not only is the mountaintop removed, but everything contained on, in, and around it—forests, birds, bears, deer, homes, cemeteries, flowers, butterflies, streams. Mountaintop removal coal mining is like using a baseball bat to remove a tooth—it may be cheaper and quicker than the dentist, but it leaves behind quite a mess.

The coal company's first step is to cut down all the trees. I look down at the fallen leaves around my boots and recognize sugar maple, tuliptree, and red oak. Ferns sprout from the rocky earth nearby.

On the walk up the mountain to this spot on the precipice, I heard the *hey there, sweetie* call of a Carolina Chickadee and the frantic laugh of a Red-bellied Woodpecker. Goldfinches flitted across the path ahead of me. I've read that Cerulean Warblers, one of the fastest-declining species of warbler in the eastern United States, could once be heard on this mountain in the spring. By this time of year, ceruleans and most other warblers have headed to points far south for the winter. I imagine their confusion when they arrive back in West Virginia, hormones revving up for the breeding season, only to discover that their mountain, the territory their ancestors have returned to for generations, is gone.

photo by Vivian Stockman

Kayford Mountain, West Virginia

Once all the trees are cut down, and the homes of birds, bears, deer, and bobcats destroyed, the coal company sometimes burns them. The billowing smoke from these funeral pyres rises hundreds of feet in the air, visible even from passing airplanes. Apparently, it's too much trouble to sell the trees for timber—the slash-and-burn techniques used to destroy the South American rainforest are much cheaper and more efficient. I remember the sadness I felt a few summers ago when I flew in a small airplane over western Maine's Appalachian mountains; most were owned by commercial logging companies, and many of the round mountaintops had been clear-cut. The destruction on Kayford Mountain makes me wish that a logging company owned this land instead of a mining company.

After the trees are burned the real business of removing the mountaintop can begin. Holes are drilled in the bare mountain, into which workers drop powerful explosives made from diesel fuel and ammonium nitrate. These explosives blast off whole sections of the mountain to expose the coal seam within. Dirt, rock, and boulders explode high into the air, sometimes showering nearby homes. Once the dust settles, heavy machinery moves in. Coal is scraped from the wrecked mountain and "overburden"—the dirt and rocks that aren't coal—is pushed into the valleys next to what had been the mountain. Streams are filled in, destroying what precious little wildlife habitat remained and contaminating the drinking water of nearby residents. Together, these valley-fills and mining sites create desolate plateaus that can never, *ever* be fully restored to healthy mountain ridges and hollows.

I peer down into the vast grey pit below me and watch the machines at work. From here, hundreds of feet above the floor of the active site, they look small, but I know that they are ridiculously over-sized. One piece of equipment, which resembles a bulldozer, slowly crawls up a makeshift road and disappears behind a cleared hill. Larry Gibson tells us that the tires on this super bulldozer are eleven feet in diameter and several Greyhound buses could fit in its front bucket. Oversized dump trucks also rumble in and out of the site, leaving clouds of grey dust in their wakes. Regular-sized pickup trucks, parked near a tiny green porta-potty, look like Matchbox toys next to the mining equipment.

I toe the loose rocks and gravel at the edge of the hole with my boot. I notice that some of the rocks around my feet are black; I bend down and pick up a dull chunk of what looks like coal. I rub its smooth, cool surface with my thumb before closing my fist around the stone. Below me, over the constant growl of the equipment, I hear the repeated beep of a truck in reverse. As I stare down at the work going on far below me, I think about the urban legend that involves dropping a penny from the top of the Empire State Building; the legend claims that a penny from that height would go right through the cement of the sidewalk below. I wonder what kind of damage my rock could cause if thrown from here. I tighten my fist and ask myself, *what would Edward Abbey do?* I try to push this question from my mind as disgust churns in my stomach. Didn't Larry Gibson say his family's cemetery, with some graves more than 200 years old, is in danger of being destroyed? Didn't he say his dogs have been shot and even hung? Cabins on his property burned? His life threatened many times? And for what—cheap energy? Have we really become that greedy?

I watch the machines creeping below me—owned by the true "ecoterrorists"—and I feel powerless. I stand before this gaping wound, this battlefield, this engineering disaster, and I am armed only with my little notebook, pen, and a stone. I feel a bit like David. But I like the way that story ended. Perhaps there is hope for us, if we take up the most effective weapons. I've chosen the ones I know how to use; you're reading them now.

photo by Vivian Stockman

Dragline, 20 stories tall

The Whole World is Watching — National Magazine & French TV Shine Spotlight on Mountaintop Massacre

by Laura Forman

US News and World Report (1997) revealed the horror of mountaintop removal mining through tragic stories from affected people and stunning aerial photography of West Virginia's "moonscapes." Here are a few of the things *US News and World Report* told the world:

"It is a fact that coal companies have been a political power in West Virginia for generations. They gave nearly $500,000 to Governor Cecil Underwood's campaign last year. A study by West Virginia Citizen action Group found that all 17 state senators elected last year got some campaign money from mining firms."

"The coal companies do not dispute that their practices are changing the landscape. But the costs are indisputable, and the damage to the landscape is startling to those who have never seen a mountain destroyed. Topographic and landscaping changes leave some regions more vulnerable to floods."

"Thirty floods have occurred in the past two years in areas where watersheds were bared and redesigned, and several people have lost their lives in such floods."

"A 1994 survey by the state Division of Water Resources found that all but 24% of the state's streams and rivers are polluted. Much of this—no one knows exactly how much—is caused by surface mining."

"The mining operation has bombarded the houses below with dust, noise, and occasional rocks."

"So rather than fight constant complaints from homeowners, Arch Coal, Inc., the mine's owner, has bought more than half of the 231 houses in Blair . . ."

"The state's weak environmental laws and lax regulators are a magnet for mining—and have made its effect more profound."

"State employment records suggest the jobs argument is not very compelling."

"Mountaintop removal accounts for only 4,317 workers in the state—less than 1% of its job force. Overall, mining employment in the state has fallen from 130,000 in the 1940s and 1950s to just 22,000 last year."

The Ohio Valley Environmental Coalition (OVEC) believes this article was an accurate and fair representation of mountaintop removal/valley fill strip mining operations in West Virginia.

In August, a television crew from France interviewed Kayford Mountain activist Larry Gibson and OVEC's Dan Kash about mountaintop removal mining. France does deep mining but not mountaintop removal strip mining. Larry took Dan Kash, French TV and local TV news stations to Kayford mountain to see how this type of mining is destroying his family's cemetery as well as the surrounding hillsides.

Blasting from nearby mining has caused many gravesites to become sunken and has destroyed grave markers. Larry said, "I used to look up on the mountains, but now I look down on them."

Perhaps the incredible scenes from West Virginia will motivate French officials to guard against this assault on the land and its people rather than welcoming it in with open arms and a fistful of tax breaks.

Will the glare of this spotlight now shining on West Virginia force our own state and local representatives to re-examine their role in this destruction of the Mountain State?

Will they recognize the need to fight these abuses against the people, the land and the wildlife?

Or will they turn away from the light, turning their backs on the people and the future of West Virginia by continuing to support the practices of the wealthy coal companies that are tearing the heart out of West Virginia?

"Like Walking Onto Another Planet"

Excerpt from interview with Jim Foster

I'm Jim Foster. I'll soon be 78 years old. I was born at what's called the old Y and O Coal camp. I grew up here and I've lived here all my life except for a brief time when I was in the United States Marine Corps. [At 17] I went to work at the coal mines and worked about ten months. [After two years in the Marines, I] came back and worked in the coal industry then until 1983 when I retired.

I'm the kind of person that has always been proud of my heritage. My father was a coal miner. I had three brothers was coal miners. . . . I feel like the work we done underground coal mining, we needed the coal to produce electricity and stuff that our nation needs. But I believe they could mine it better without destroying the environment like they're doing with mountaintop removal.

When I was just a young man, when I first saw coal mining through strip mining—which was a disaster to me—I'll never forget what my dad said. He said, "Son, this is the ruination of our state if they allow this strip mining to go on like that. They can't do that in these mountains and survive." Which was true. I knew that. But I've said I'm proud my dad didn't live to see this mountaintop removal because if he had, he would absolutely . . . it would have broke his heart. If he knew it today, he would turn over in his grave.

I believe they can mine the coal and do it underground and not do the damage to the environment like they're doing. The only reason they're doing it the way they're doing it with mountaintop removal is because they can do it with dynamite and machinery instead of working men. They don't want to pay men a decent wage to mine the coal—they want to use mountaintop removal.

One person can't do anything, but if everybody would open their eyes to the fact of what's happening and do something, stand up to them, they might listen to them.

Probably after I'm dead and gone they'll pass on new laws that will outlaw this. I just wish they had done it sooner so that some of the generations that's coming on ahead of me could have a better place to live in.

Christians for the Mountains

by Denise Giardina

When God created heaven and earth, he looked at his handiwork and declared it "good." Each act of creation received this word of divine satisfaction. As time passed, only one part of God's creation became the subject of disappointment and anger—ourselves. But after the destruction of the Flood, God declared he would not repeat this act. As Christians, we believe that God even took human form in order to redeem us. The apostle Paul believed that redemption extended to the whole of creation. ("The creation itself will be set free from its bondage to decay . . ." Romans 8:21)

Throughout time God has shown his continued love for creation. But God seems to have a special love for mountains. Time and again, when God wants to meet Man, he chooses mountains. Abraham was asked to sacrifice Isaac on a mountain. Moses was called to receive the Ten Commandments upon a mountain, and God showed him the Promised Land from a mountain. Jesus preached his greatest sermon upon a mountain. Monks in medieval England and Ireland saw mountains as "thin places." Places where it is especially easy to pray and communicate with God. Psalm 68 even speaks of God having a mountain for his abode.

As a beloved part of creation, mountains themselves have been seen as participating in praising and thanking God. In the Psalms and elsewhere, the mountains and hills are described as skipping for job. If we may speak to God from atop a mountain, the mountains themselves also sing praise to their Creator in their own special language.

Mountains have also given us enduring spiritual metaphors. Paul, in his first letter to the Corinthians, speaks of a faith that can move mountains (I Cor. 13:2), though he goes on to add that without love, such faith is meaningless. Paul here is speaking of faith so strong it can accomplish the impossible. Moving mountains was meant to stay just that—impossible.

What then can we say about mountaintop removal? First we must acknowledge that man has indeed developed the capability to move mountains. We have that capability—but should we exercise it? Clearly God did not mean that we should, for to literally move a mountain makes the metaphor meaningless.

But mountaintop removal does far more spiritual damage than the destruction of language. The Appalachian Mountains, according to geologists, are among the oldest in the world. This means they are among the first mountains God created. The beautiful Appalachian Mountains are a balm to the soul. Their destruction speaks of the soul's sickness.

If God loves mountains so much, and scripture is clear that he does, how must we grieve him when we destroy them? When scripture bids us look up to the hills, from whence comes out help, how may we when those hills are gone? Where is hope or comfort then, when the sings of hope given by God, the mountains, have been leveled?

Psalm 24 tells us that the earth, and the fullness thereof, belongs to the Lord. Woe on us if we continue to destroy what is the Lord's. but the woe, the shame, is for more than just disobeying God. When we destroy the beautiful, the sacred mountains, we reject God's gift. It is a gift near to the heart of God. To destroy the mountains is to spit in the face of God. It must break his heart.

photo by Delilah O'Haynes

A Tennessee Lake

This Land Will Never Be For Sale

by Larry Gibson

reprinted by permission of OVEC

My name is Larry Gibson. I really didn't start having violence until I surveyed my own land. The land has been in the family for over 220 years and had never been surveyed by anybody in the family except me. So when I did survey the land, I found that it had always been surveyed in behalf of the oil company, a utility company, a coal company—but never in behalf of the people. I started forcing 'em back on the boundaries where they was supposed to be and that's when the violence started. And the first few years, I couldn't even get the law to come up there because my land sits in three counties. Then when I got to be friends with [former WV Congressman] Ken Hechler, then and only then did I start getting support from the local officials. The police, not the state troopers. But up there, it's in the wilderness, sits by itself. Most times when things happen, ain't nobody can help anyhow. It's done and over with before anybody can even be told about it, much less get ready for it.

There's people that's angry about what happens. But you got to be not only angry, you gotta be willin' to do something, you know? I been fightin' for my place for 18 years now. You can't go into a situation where people are gathering for the first time and saying "We've had 118 acts of violence," yet they're just now beginning to get involved. You can't do that. You gotta tell people something positive—but you can't make it easy and tell them that nothing's gonna happen to them because there's always the potential.

That [coal company] fellow was on TV the other day—he's the one I met with back in '92. And he told me my land was worth a million dollars an acre to the coal company then. And he turns around and offers $140,000 for it. You know, it was like we didn't know the difference! Even if we wanted to sell, he was talking to us like they were really gonna do us a favor. "We're gonna help y'all out, make a generous offer to you." And he'd just told me it was worth over a million dollars.

Then when he said that, I said, "The land'll never be for sale. You can have my right arm, but you'll never get the land." So he said, "Well, you know, you're the island and we are the ocean. You set in the middle of 187,000 acres of coal company land. You're the only thing we don't own between here and the Virginia border." I had my family members—seven of us—there for that meeting and it just didn't make no sense.

That man said, "We don't give a damn about the people up the holler. We don't care about anybody, anything. All we want is the coal and that's it." And up to this point, they've proved their point. They don't care about the people. The most endangered species we have in West Virginia besides our own people that's bein' displaced out of the mountains and the hollers is the deep miners. People say, "Why don't they say somethin'?" Well, who they gonna say it to? The United Mine Workers is no longer a viable union, all they do is take money from people. They don't do anything for the people. Who you gonna go to? Up my holler when I was a boy, we had 25,000 miners. There was nothin' that went out of that holler without the union's control. And if you worked for a scab outfit, you didn't tell anybody. Now there's nothin' that goes out my holler that's not under company control, and if you work for a union you don't tell anybody. I see a day when the violence is gonna come back like it did on the Blair Mountain battle.

I've been through the experience of bein' shot at a numerous amount of times because of my stand on what I believe in. People say, "Why don't you just sell?" They've offered me seven times the amount of acreage as what I've got for my place. But then the land they offered me—my people never walked on it. It's been turned over. You can't put anything on it, can't grow anything on it.

The other day I was thinkin' about somethin' I could probably do that would give me the same amount in respect of breakin' the law as what the coal company's doin' now. I've been called a terrorist. I've been called an extremist. I've been called a radical. And the very people around me, they've not been typed extremist or radical.

Recently I was told that we should start workin' with the union again. Well, it was a union site on Princess Beverly right beside of me. The violence didn't start toward me heavily until [UMWA President] Cecil Roberts endorsed mountain top removal—that was in 1999—and made reference to me as an extremist radical. Well, my dad was workin' in the mine when Roberts started as a boy. He knew me all my life, and yet he got on national TV, on the Capitol steps in front of 1,500 miners, in 1999 and made reference to me as an extremist radical from out-of-state!

And so that's when the violence started. That's when it really escalated. I was havin' trouble before, but I didn't really know what I was goin' into. Now recently they tell me that my land is now—since George Bush got into office—worth $450 million dollars. And they told me six months ago that by time he gets out of office it will be escalated up to $650 million.

photo by Delilah O'Haynes

Kayford Mountain – the view from Larry Gibson's property

So I tell people that we have the very best President that we've ever had in the history of mankind right now. I'll be in front of a big crowd at a university or a college, or a big church association or somethin' and you could hear a pin hit the carpet because they're gaspin', tryin' to get their breath about what I just said. And what I meant, and when they let me finish what I'm sayin' before they wanna hang me, is the fact that this man has undone every environmental gain we've made over the last 150 years, just in the six years of his office. And in another two years, we'll never live long enough, because we'll have more of them little Georges runnin' around for the next 50, 60 years. The grip that he's gonna have us in, the vice that he's gonna have us in—doesn't really matter whether we're right or not. Like a man told me the other day, we're gonna be *dead right*.

I had some people come to see me this past weekend, and you'll be amazed where they come from and you'll be amazed what they said. They come from Israel. And all the problems they're havin' in Israel right now, with the bombin's and everything—and they turned and looked at me and said they feel sorry for *me*.

We lost about 80, well, close to a hundred headstones in the family cemetery, because every time the coal company would blast, they'd blast debris over into the cemetery. It would bust some of the headstones, turn some of 'em over. Then they'd send a crew of men over to clean 'em up. And then the old sandstone headstones that had carving on 'em, we caught 'em actually throwing them away, destroying them as well. And the simple reason behind that was to prove that we didn't have as many graves there on the ground as we had. And so if they could reclaim some of the gravesites, well, the mountain had 39 seams of coal. There's a lot of wealth underneath there.

But the thing is, that cemetery has been undermined now by nine different companies we have names to, and six others that we don't, over the last 125 years. I'm just doin' this because it's my right to fight for the resting place of my people, but more than likely the people are not even there. And you walk through my cemetery, you can actually see where the underground mine is because the graves are droppin'. We now have mine cracks developin' and a big hole developin'. And on the other family cemetery across the ridge we have mine cracks right through the graves that's three and four feet wide, that you can see down in and there's no casket, no body—all that's left is a headstone. And these people that come from Israel, they said, "You mean the coal company doesn't have any respect for the cemetery?" I said, "The coal company don't have respect for the livin', much less the dead."

When I was a kid, our place was like a wonderland. People used to make fun of me and say I was my father's retarded son—they'd call me that, you know? One of the things they couldn't understand was that I was always able to get close to the wild animals. I'd go out in the woods and come home with a bobcat or a squirrel or a coon. One time I was helpin' my dad fix a swing, hang a swing, and I had my bib overalls on. I was settin' there and squirmin' and bouncin' around. My dad asked in a kind of angry way what I was doin' and a frog started jumpin' out of my pocket.

We never had toys. The only toys we had was in the Spiegel catalog when we went to the bathroom. But it was a wonderland, you know? You could walk through the forest. You could hear the animals. The woods like to talk to you. You could feel a part of Mother Nature. In other words, everywhere you looked there was life. Now you put me on the same ground where I walked, and the only thing you can feel is the vibration of dynamite or heavy machinery. No life, just dust.

How was it when I was a kid? I'll put it to you this way—when they took me to Cleveland, that's the first time that I ever knew I was poor. *They* told me I was poor. Me? I thought I was the richest person in the world. I didn't want for anything. I'd get out in the woods, and on my way, if I was hungry I'd pick my apples. I had a pocket knife I always carried—I'd cut cucumbers up in somebody's garden. Or I'd get chased out of somebody's apple tree. I'd get berries along the way. Pawpaws—I loved pawpaws. And gooseberries.

All these things are no longer there. Now they're forcin' wild boar into my area, and deer into my area, and there wasn't any kind of animal like that when I was a kid. Mostly all small game and an occasional bear. Every other year or so we'd see a bear. Now they're forcin' the bears in on me. A bear needs 50 acres to feed on and now there's nothin' for 'em.

In my childhood, I had a pigeon. I'd come out of my cabin and no matter where I went, he was either flyin' over my head or settin' on my shoulder. One time I had a hawk. I named him Fred. For the longest time he was around, then all of a sudden one day he didn't show up. I had a bobcat, and I had a three-legged fox that got caught in a trap. I kept it until it got healed and then it wouldn't leave. I wouldn't trade my childhood for all the fancy fire trucks in the world that the kids had. Nor toys.

It was a hard way, but it didn't seem so hard because it's the only way we knew. What would you walk four or five miles to school for? Because that's the only thing you knew. Now you can't get a kid to go to the front door to catch the bus. I didn't see a TV 'til

I was 13. Didn't talk on a phone 'til I was 14. Now when my kids was growin' up, I'd threaten to take the TV off 'em. "How we gonna make it for a whole month without a TV, Dad?" they'd say. That's the problem today—we ain't one with the earth no more.

I don't know what the answer is as far as what's happenin'. Destroyin' all the environment—all the streams. When I was a kid, down at the bottom of the mountain, I could get crawdads, pick 'em up out of the water with my toes. Now nothin' lives in the water. Nothin' lives on the land. What they've done is irreversible. You can't bring it back. I was just asked this question last week when I was in Tennessee. A lady said, "We've been readin' where you've been fightin' for eighteen years. We'd like to know what keeps you goin'." I just told her I was right. You know, if you're right, you're right. There's no other answer. There's one thing I was taught at a very young age, as a boy livin' in the coalfields. We didn't know the United States President, but we knew the United Mine Workers' President. In other words, we was organized as young people. And that's the way I grew up. Organized. You learn to fight back and you fight back. You have to fight back. That's the way it was, and that's the way it is for me today. And that's the way I try to reach out to people, to show 'em. There is a sayin' I've lived by all my life, "If you don't stand for somethin', you'll fall for anything." That's not an original statement, somebody else came up with it. But the thing is, it's true.

I came through here four or five months ago tryin' to find some family of mine that was in Cleveland with me when I was a boy. Ain't no sign of anybody that I used to know. And that's the way it is all through the coalfields. We've lost 25 percent of the population because of mountain top removal. Remember I said a while ago, we used to have 25,000 miners in my holler. Now we got 500, and they do the work of 25,000....

People need to grab a hold of what they've got, or once the coal company gets through there'll be nothin' left. This ritual of takin' our men to mine for coal—there's not one life worth losin' for coal. As of 1997, we've lost 200,000 men to black lung and cave-ins alike. We lose men every year. And this disaster we just had [at the Sago mine], now people are lookin' at it. Now people are passin' laws. Every time somethin' happens like the Buffalo Creek they pass laws. But then they twist the laws and they still break the laws. Every law that's ever been written has been written in a coal miner's blood.

What I want to say now at the end of this is to encourage people to stand up against oppression and speak for theirself. Because if they're waitin' for the people that's doin' it to 'em to speak for 'em, it's never gonna happen. They're gonna keep takin' and takin' and takin'. Folks have to get in their head that the people that's doin' it to 'em don't' care about 'em. They have to care about theirself. They have to take control of their own destiny. Whether it's a coal company or a chemical company or what, they're not gonna do it for the people. The people have to do it for theirself.

photo by Vivian Stockman

Southern West Virginia

Paw Paw

by Stephen Godfrey

The black lung bit him to the core.
Stripped him down to skin and bone.
I remember your big hands, calloused,
But loving to a little boy.

I never heard you complain;
Your dignity was all you had left.
Wheezing, coughing, spitting up
The lung for seven years.

I focus on the picture of you
And Maw Maw on my coffee table.
Young and in spats up to your knees;
Vigorous and strong was your Irish face.

Wine Oak Coal and Coke Company
Was one of the mines you
Crawled on your knees; to
Fill the mule cart with tonnage.

A three mile trek up Arista
Moutain to catch a ride
To the mine was a daily event.
You worked in other mines in
Tralee and Garwood, Wyoming County.

Paw Paw, you're my hero,
I would say to you if I could.
The coal company sucked the air
Out of your lungs, and did not
Want to pay a penny.

My Life Is On The Line

reprinted with permission of OVEC

My name's Maria Gunnoe. I'm from Bob White on Route 85 in Boone County, West Virginia, and mountain top removal moved into my backyard in 2000. Since then, I've lost two access bridges, the use of my water, about five acres of land. There's 13 landslides between me and the toe of the landfill behind me. Each time it rains these landslides move. All depending on how much rain we get, sometimes they can move as much as five feet in one day. You know that eventually they're gonna wash out, and when they do, I will have another major washout there at my home.

Since 2000, I've been flooded seven times. One time I was flooded with no rain…blue skies and just barely any clouds at all in the sky…and the stream coming through my property just came up. It came up about three feet. By the time I called the DEP [WV Department of Environmental Protection] and made the proper complaints and reports, the water had subsided. The DEP said there was no evidence of what had happened and therefore it was OK.

And with that, I'm gonna add that the DEP doesn't allow citizens to take samples of the water that runs by their house. So I mean if I had run out there and got a sample, it would have been nothing more than my sample. The DEP is not there for the citizens, they're there for the coal companies, and they enable the coal companies. In some cases they even lie to the citizens in order to continue the work on the mountaintop removal site. I've been lied to many times. I've had five DEP agents stand and look at me and tell me an eroded mountain wasn't eroded. I have pictures and a lot of proof showing that it's eroded. It's like they were programmed to say—no matter what I said—that it was not eroded.

They just will not admit the fact that the mountains behind me is crumbling in on my home. The mountains are slipping into the hollow and in turn, it's washing by me, and [it's] flooding the people across from me. Everyone downstream from where that mountaintop removal site is gets flooded and their wells are contaminated. My well is contaminated. Can't drink my water. I buy on average about $250 worth of water a month, and that's on a slow month. The WV

American Water Company's wantin' $31,000 to put water in to me. And that's only 500 feet worth of water line. They want $31,000 for that. I can't afford that, of course.

And the financial aspects of what these catastrophic floods has done to our lives is just unbelievable. Lookin' back on it, myself and my husband had real good jobs, workin' full time, doin' the life thing—you know, livin' life. And then this flood thing started and we was just bein' completely wiped out. And in response to all the floods, and to the coal company's claims that this was an "act of God" takin' place in my back yard, I began organizing other people here in the neighborhood. I got to lookin' around, and it seemed that the people around me was bein' affected or were in line to be affected by this same mountain top removal site. Doing this, I've also educated myself on mountain top removal in the regional area, in the Appalachian region. And I've been workin' consistently for the past five years—locally I've been workin' for seven years—on the issue of mountaintop removal and what it's doin' to our communities.

photo by Maria Gunnoe

Erosion resulting from MTR flooding

People around here are swiggin' down contaminated water all day long, every day. The health affects are sometimes long-term. It's usually pancreatic cancer or some kind of liver disease, or kidney stones, gall stones—digestive tract problems. And then, too, people's breathing. The blasting is killin' people—just smotherin' them to death through breathin' all of the dust. The computers and electronics and stuff in my house stay completely packed up with black coal dirt and rock dust together. Why do they expect us to just take this? It's not gonna happen down at the state capital. I mean they're not gonna go up there and blast off the top of a mountain in the background of the Capitol.

Through my organizing, I've met quite a bit of....I guess you could call it opposition. I've had my children get harassed. I've got a 15-year-old boy and an 11-year-old girl. I have a 15-year-old boy that looks like a 30-year-old man—he's very big. He's been harassed by grown men. They call him tree-hugger and just generally say things to him that's not nice. My son just takes it and goes—he's a real trooper.

Before I began doing this, let me say, I did talk to my kids about it. My children don't want to leave where they're at, and that gives us one choice. That gives us the choice of fightin' to stay. And we talked about it. When all this first come up, I really felt it was in our best interest to leave, but we were unable to do so. The property's been devalued so bad that you can't get nothin' out of it to move forward with your life. And you can't hardly walk off and leave everything you've got. So that's pretty much the point that we're at now.

And I see this happening throughout the communities in southern West Virginia, and then too in Tennessee and Kentucky. And it's wrong, you know? I mean it's flat-out wrong to do people like this. If you react, the strip miners will cut you short every time. If you lash out and say, "Why are you destroyin' my home?" they'll look at you and say, "Well, I gotta have a job."

And they will verbally attack you in front of other people in the convenience store and say things to you that's just completely and totally unnecessary. They will say things to you that really instigate you, and makes you—considering all we go through here day to day—just want to reach out and grab 'em and shake the daylights out of 'em! I wanna say, "How can you do me like this in the name of jobs? How can you do me and my family like this and expect us to sit by and just let you do it?"

photo by Maria Gunnoe

Erosion resulting from MTR flooding

    One thing about West Virginia people is we're not the kind to give up and walk away. If we was the kind to give up and walk away, we would never have settled this area years and years ago. Because this was a very rough terrain—a very rough life here. But people loved it—people like my great-grandmother, people like my grandfather before me. They loved this land, and tended this land. It's land that wasn't meant to be developed. It's a special land. God put it way up high so they'd leave it alone. I've had people to tell me that God put the coal there for us to mine. I have to disagree with that. He buried it because it's so daggone nasty!

    The coal companies like to say that the mountain top land is just useless land, and that's not true. How can they say that? That's insane to me. My family growin' up—my grandfather had mountain corn fields and grew corn up in these mountains. And you know, that's our survival. The mountains are literally our survival. And now as long as you're driving through here on the paved road, you're OK, but if you get off that paved road on one side or the other, you're gonna be stopped. You're not allowed into these mountains any more! How can they tell the mountain people that they're no longer allowed in the mountains? That's not right. They're taking away everything that puts us together as a people. And they're expecting *the wrong people* to sit back and take this.

We're not stupid by no means. There's a lot of very, very intelligent people here that can't read and write, but they're not stupid. They're brilliant in their own sense of the word. They have intelligence that's not taught in college. These people are the people I grew up with—the people I love. And these are people that I won't walk away from. And I would probably stand up to the biggest, strongest, most evil power in the world in order to protect them and to protect their rights to retire in their homes—and to protect their rights to be who they are in the communities they're in.

In doing this, I've had a little bit of everything done to me. I've been accused of all kinds of stuff. I've had sand put in my gas tank—cost $1,200 to keep my truck on the road. And you know, in this kind of area, if they ground your vehicle, you're grounded! You're stopped right there, dead in your tracks. I'm 25 miles from the nearest town, so that really slowed me down for quite a while. Teachers in the schools make comments to my kids. It's not their place to tell my children that their water isn't poisoned by coal, when my children know they can't drink their water. I've had my tires cut, my dog shot. People spit on my truck all the time—big, gross tobacco juice spit.

One of my dogs was shot and left in the parkin' lot where my kids catch the school bus. This was my daughter's dog. She actually nursed this dog when he was a baby—he was fed a bottle and was a little spoiled. But this was her dog, it wasn't my dog. My aunt, luckily, worked at the Post Office. She called me and told me that a dog was layin' over there dead, and instead of takin' the kids to the bus stop, I just took them on to school. Then when I came back and confirmed that it was our dog, we were just completely devastated. He was a three-year-old baby, really. He was very close to the family. He had veered back onto the mountain top removal site. The last time I seen him, that was the direction he was headed. When they first came in up there, they used to feed my dogs. I kind of feel like they baited him in for the kill.

photo by Maria Gunnoe

Erosion resulting from MTR flooding

Then I had a dog shot at the back of my house. It was tied at the back of my house. It's gotten to the point I can't leave my dogs untied because somebody might kill 'em. Well, I had the dog tied at the back of my house and he was shot right in the top of the head. This was within thirty feet of my bedroom window. There's a lot of trains goes by where I live at, so they could've done it while a train was goin' by and I wouldn't have heard it. Had it been a small caliber gun, I wouldn't have heard it. They know that. They know how to get you. By killing off your animals, that opens them a way to get in your place without people knowin' it.

The people in these communities, they feel the blasting, they see the trucks on the road runnin' over top of their family.

They see what's going on, but they don't see what it looks like from the sky. Seein' what it looks like from the sky *scares* you. It scares you real bad to come home to it. When it rains here, we all get flooded. And then the coal companies, they care so much! After five acres of my land and my life washed down the stream, the coal company engineer came into my front yard and said that this was "an act of God!"

You know, the night when this wall of water was comin' down through the hollow at me, I run to the mountain. But the mountain was slidin' and I couldn't go there. I couldn't get out, the streams had me and my family surrounded. I literally hit my knees, and I prayed for everything I was worth! And there *was* an act of God took place that night. But not the one they claimed. And that was the same claim they made after they killed 125 people in the Buffalo Creek flood. I lost family in the Buffalo Creek flood. My father was a rescuer in the Buffalo Creek flood. So that incident was very close to our family.

To see what come off that mountain, and to know what it had been like for 37 years, well, it's a big eye-opener to realize what a dramatic difference the mountain top removal makes in everything! I mean, everything around these strip sites is constantly erodin', and there's always water runnin' in all different directions. The DEP calls that "streams meandering." They were never streams before—now they're streams! This process it's tearin' my property all to pieces, and I have no rights over my property. The only right I have over my property is the right to pay taxes on it! I have no control over what's goin' on. The coal company has tore it all to pieces. It looks awful. Our place had always been pretty much handmanicured. My father and my grandfather before me took very good care of it. We had fruit trees and just an abundance of food producing plants right there next to where I lived at. Our land has always been tended in a way that it took care of us. Now that's no longer the case. Our soil's contaminated. A garden that we'd gardened for all the thirty-seven years that I've been there is now covered with coal slurry. You can't grow food in that. My yard was completely washed out. My fruit trees are gone. My nut trees are gone. I woke up the next morning and looked at this massive trench in my front yard and just really…it took me three days to absorb it. I went from crying—sobbing—to being *very mad*. This was three years ago, and I'm still mad. And honestly, I'm a little madder than I was then because I realize how many tentacles this evil has. It goes all the way to Washington, D.C. And if I have to go up against it and fight for my home, I'm goin' against it. It's even the United States government. And that alone is pretty intimidating. But at the same time, so is that wall of water sittin' back up on that mountain waitin' for me.

I don't think I've ever run up against anything that intimidated me that bad. Keeps me up at night. Keeps my kids up at night. And that's when you know how powerful the intimidation of these waters are. When you get to the point that you ain't had ten hours of sleep in a week, and it comes time to lay down and go to sleep and it starts rainin'…and you don't go to sleep…well!

People look at you different ways. There's a lot of people here who support what I do. But there's others who drive in here every day for their jobs, and given a choice, they'd run over me in a heartbeat. They'd do anything they could to get rid of me. But I know I'm bein' effective and I know I'm makin' a change. And with that change will come the intimidation factors. But it just doesn't work—there's nothin' more intimidating than what they've already put me through. So—bring it on.

I'm settin' there on my porch, which is my favorite place in the whole world, by the way—I'd rather be on my front porch than any other place in the world and I've been to a lot of places. As it stands right now, with the new permits I saw last week, they're gonna blast off the mountain I look at when I look off my front porch. And I get to set and watch that happen, and I'm not supposed to react. Don't react, just set there and take it. They're gonna blast away my horizon, and I'm expected to say, "It's OK. It's for the good of all."

Am I willing to sacrifice myself and my kids, and my family and my health and my home for everybody else? No—I don't owe nobody nothin'. It's all I can do to take care of my family and my place. It was all I could do before I started fightin' mountain top removal. Now that I'm fightin' mountaintop removal, it makes it nearly impossible. But at the same time, *my life is on the line*. My kids' lives are on the line. You don't give up on that and walk away. You don't throw up your hands and say, "Oh, it's OK, you feed me three million tons of blasting material a day. *That's fine*, I don't mind. It's for the betterment of all." I can't say that there's anything out there that I'm willin' to risk myself and my kids for. Nothin'. No amount of money, no amount of energy, no amount of anything. If it come down to it, we could live up under a rock cliff with what the good Lord above give us. And we could *live* like that, as long as we got clean water, clean air, and a healthy environment. We can take care of ourselves from there. But when they contaminate our water, our air, and our environment we're gonna die no matter what we do.

That's it.

photo by Delilah O'Haynes

Bluestone Lake, West Virginia

photo by Bob Gates

Valley Fill Erosion

photo by Delilah O'Haynes

Erosion After Clear-Cut Logging

Two Letters

by Jewele Haynes

I have lived on Herald road, outside Coeburn, VA, in beautiful southwest, VA mountains for 37½ years. In the surrounding area and towns, mining companies and equipment, coal hauling trucks and the ever-present fine black dust is part of the everyday scenery along with the lush green beauty of this area. Coal mining keeps the economy going in southwestern Virginia. Coal mining has also destroyed many of the natural water supplies on private owned land. Natural water supplies (wells and ponds) on private farmland has made it possible for landowners to raise livestock. Many of those landowners, couple of them friends of mine, have stopped raising livestock because the ponds and wells on their property went dry years ago. The ponds and wells going dry was not due to a drought, it was due to coal mining under the property or under adjacent property which re-directed the natural water sources. This is one of those consequences which is a direct result of our economy and could not be foreseen. No one really owns water streams or air currents. The ponds and underground streams had been in the mountains since their creation. For that farmer who owns land, which had been in his family for generations, and the natural water is redirected away from his land, it is a bitter reality from which there is no recovery. So, life goes on and history is documented.

Letter to the Editor, *Coalfield Progress*

I read the article on the possibility of wind farms in Wise County. I applaud this and its rapid beginning. Wind turbines are truly gentle giants who use the upper level wind currents to provide electricity with no smoke, no fumes and no poison gasses. One wind farm in Oklahoma with 210 wind turbines provides total electricity for 83,000 homes. Opponents will say "what if a bird smashes into a propeller." How many birds are now smashed by moving planes and automobiles? The turbines are stationary towers. Opponents will say "they'll destroy the landscape." I believe they are beautiful and

would destroy the landscape no more than power and phone poles and lines. With wind providing much of the electric power, my grandchildren may have opportunities for a much cleaner, healthier Wise County. We don't wish to live without electricity, so why not create it in the most natural, accessible and healthy way?
— Jewele Haynes, Coeburn, Virginia

photo by Delilah O'Haynes

Virginia Landscape

Four Voices from the *Herald Dispatch* –
reprinted with permission

Bill Price: Mountaintop mining adds little to WV economy – Nov 19, 2007

I lived in the coalfields of Southern West Virginia for more than 35 years. My father was a miner, and I'm fully aware that coal put food on our table and clothes on our backs. So, I get incensed when people say that to be against mountaintop removal mining is to be "against coal."

Let's face it. Mountaintop removal is not the type of mining that brings huge amounts of jobs to the communities where the mining is happening. The current controversy over the Jupiter Mine is an example. If we enforce the law and stop dumping fill in the valley, then we might lose 39 jobs. But if that coal were being mined by conventional methods instead of blowing up the mountain, then that would generate around 200 jobs.

I'm not saying that the 39 jobs are not important; certainly they are. But compared to times past, mining is not bringing the jobs to West Virginia that it used to. The West Virginia Coal Association would point out that the employment figures do not include other jobs at gas stations, carryouts, grocery stores, etc. But those types of jobs, if indeed they are linked to coal, have also suffered due to the documented decrease in mining jobs.

One only has to look at the poverty rates, high school dropout rates and other figures to determine that the coal regions of West Virginia fall behind the rest of the nation. But the industry continues to tout this as a jobs versus the environment issue. And it's simply not true.

People such as Maria Gunnoe and many others recognize that our past is not our future. For that, they need to be applauded, not threatened and ridiculed. Every year, more and more people recognize that if we are going to have a sustainable economy in West Virginia, we must transition from coal to a new energy economy. Groups such as the Ohio Valley Environmental Coalition, West Virginia Highlands, Coal River Mountain Watch, Sierra Club and others work every day to help facilitate that transition in such a way as to ensure a bright future for our children and grandchildren.

We are not supportive of the immediate closing of all coal mining. We do, in the spirit of community health, safety and economic well being, support the abolition of mountaintop removal mining.

The people I work with across this state are advocating for cleaner forms of energy. We feel that the economic future of this state would be better served by the jobs that would come with renewable and sustainable energy. And the number of those jobs would be significant.

A recent study by the Perryman Group estimates that transitioning to an economy based on renewable energy would create 13,898 jobs in West Virginia, including 2,200 new manufacturing jobs and 2,013 new construction jobs. An additional $884 million of economic activity would occur in West Virginia.

We have a choice. We can continue to listen to the coal industry scare tactics of economic doom unless we continue along the path that has not worked. Or we can listen to forward-thinking community leaders who are advocating for real job growth and environmental sanity where people can breathe clean air and drink clean water.

I believe that we can have good-paying, long-lasting, union-organized jobs where we don't have to destroy our communities in order to prosper. I would say to the workers at Jupiter and other mines in West Virginia, come join in that effort. Join us in working toward a better West Virginia.

Bill Price is environmental justice resource coordinator for the Sierra Club in Charleston.

Melvin L. Tyree: We must save Earth for the next generation – Oct 30, 2007

This letter is written in reference to the Oct. 14 letter, "Mining destroys God's mountains." Whether one chooses to believe Creation is God's gift to humanity or if Creation is a wondrous accident of nature, the present generation has a spiritual and moral obligation to preserve that gift for the generations that follow us.

This obligation to be proper stewards of Creation transcends tomorrow's paycheck, next week's mortgage or even next year's corporate profit returns for Big Coal's CEOs. It is in essence the world we leave our children. Nothing is more important than that.

We are now seeing the impacts to their future. Our arctic ice cap is being threatened with irreversible melting due to the carbon dioxide we so foolishly emit into our atmosphere from burning billions of tons of coal and petroleum every year. If this practice continues for just another eight or 10 years, that ice cap will be destined for oblivion. And with it, Nature's fury will be unleashed upon the United States like nothing that has been seen since our species evolved.

If we are so stupid as to continue mining and burning coal like there is no tomorrow, no tomorrow is exactly what Nature will give us. Without that ice cap, ocean currents will change, prevailing weather patterns will shift and our arctic air will no longer be cooled from the natural radiator of the Arctic.

This is it. We must decide now if we're going to be "Friends of Coal" and go out in a crazed carbon-fueled blaze of glory, or dig our heels in, turn the ship into the wind and fight for the generations that follow us.

—Hurricane, W.Va.

Briana McElfish: Residents deserve better than coal

One recent weekend, I visited an awesome example of what our fossil fuel dependence costs us. At Kayford Mountain I saw not just the destruction of the mountains but heard from people whose health and livelihood are threatened every day by mountaintop removal coal mining.

Mingo County fought three years just to get drinkable water after theirs was poisoned in the industry's attempt to dispose of coal waste, and now communities across the state are facing the same plight, including a range of cancers, liver, kidney and reproductive diseases.

Residents in Boone County are subjected to so much coal dust that some who have never entered a mine suffer from black lung disease. I watched children play in the leaves and realized their young bodies are being exposed to the consequences of mountaintop removal pollution. They are West Virginia's future. They deserve so much better.

In order to end this devastation, we must end mountaintop removal and ensure a just transition for workers into a new clean energy economy so that West Virginia may prosper and our people may thrive. Conservation and renewable energy help more than just birds and trees; after all, who's dying for your cheap energy?
—Huntington, WV

Julia Bonds: Effects of strip mining – Nov 6, 2007

We are not against responsible underground coal mining. Coal is a finite resource and will end sooner than later. The use of coal greatly contributes to global warming, climate crisis. While we will be in a transition to renewable energy, responsible underground mining will be the only acceptable option.

We talk of the horror of more coal mined, we mean irresponsible mining, strip mining and sludge dams. Surface mine workers hurt the underground miners the first day a surface mine opened. Coal mining wouldn't be under such scrutiny and in such trouble today if it wasn't for the horror, destruction and poison of strip mining. Most mining lawsuits wouldn't be filed if it weren't for mountaintop removal strip mining and sludge dams. —Rock Creek, WV

photo courtesy of Kentuckians For The Commonwealth

Mountaintop Removal Mining in Kentucky

Appalachia, America's Fourth World

by Chris Irwin

originally published in *Tennessee Mountain Defender*, 4th ed., 2008

My grandmother once told that the rest of the country viewed Appalachia as America's "fourth world." By this, she explained, that practices which would not be acceptable for a third world country, are somehow considered acceptable in Appalachia.

Later, while in the Peace Corps in Africa, I came to this same conclusion. My job was in natural resources management (NRM) and I took part in significant erosion control programs in the West African nation of Guinea. Millions of aid dollars from USAID and the World Bank, along with funding from other international agencies, were used to fund watershed and forest preservation programs—to keep the streams clear of sediment, to preserve the soil and reforest the land.

After the Peace Corps I lived in Northern California where I did a tour in Americorps doing Chinook salmon habitat restoration. I saw multiple agencies spend millions trying to protect California's streams and forest against sedimentation of streams, poor logging practices, sloppy mining, and destructive industries.

It was after these experiences that I came home to Tennessee and found air pollution that at times rivals that of Mexico City. I witnessed the US Forest Service clear cutting Appalachian forests. TDOT was blasting roads through the countryside, burning highland watersheds, turning streams into chocolate sludge, and causing dust storms from the resulting dirt.

I soon discovered that the Tennessee River I played in as a child is the most heavy metal contaminated river in the world due to the mercury and witches brew (pardon witches) streaming from Oak Ridge, the heart of the American nuclear weapons productions complex. The Holston River wasn't faring much better, having become an industrial drainage ditch with over 200 companies issued discharge permits. I discovered federal and state agencies jumping over each other to hand out strip mine permits as fast as they could, regardless of the result of this and cannot help but contrast it with my experiences in Africa and California.

It all came back to what my grandmother told me. Appalachia really is the fourth world. The rest of the nation does things to our land and people in direct opposition of what our agencies tell people to do overseas. The very practices I was paid to combat in Africa and California are openly encouraged of corporations in Tennessee and Appalachia in general.

photo by Bob Gates

Erosion from MTR Flooding, Lyburn, WV

It's as if corporations feel entitled to come to Appalachia, take our land, clear-cut our forests, bring all the toxic industries to our region, strip mine, and in general act as if they are the colonialist British come to occupy our land. The sheer arrogance of their swagger as they blow up our mountains for coal is staggering. Somehow banks, our government, and corporations have perpetuated the idea that it's acceptable to destroy Appalachian land, and occasionally to steal it. It's acceptable to blow up highland watersheds in Appalachia, yet we spend millions to keep people from doing it in the third world—and elsewhere in America.

Any region or people portrayed negatively are easier to exploit. The mass media and cultural portrayal of Appalachia is a tool enabling a few to extract our resources and abuse our rivers, streams and people at the expense of the many. It's a tactic commonly used in colonialism.

Redneck, hillbilly, inbred, racist, over-all wearing, ignorant, intolerant, violent, dumb, slow, slovenly, speakers of fractured English, illiterate, feuding, vicious, snake handling, speaking in tongues, in deep poverty, and naïve.

What region in America am I describing?

You know already. Negative stereotypes reinforce negative beliefs about the Appalachian Mountains and her people. The source of these images is obvious—the corporate owned mass media.

Who profits from the character assassination of Appalachia?

What I found is that it's the same people who profit from the physical destruction of Appalachia. It's the strip mine owners, the coal plant owners, the nuclear power industry, and the nuclear weapons industry—simply put, those who pollute and destroy our land and profit from that destruction the most.

Portraying the people of Appalachia as stupid, ignorant, and inbred somehow makes it acceptable to turn streams bright orange and to blow up entire mountains and destroy highland watersheds forever. We are naïve, so of course companies—and at times the federal government—have felt entitled to seize whole Appalachian towns. We don't know how to take care of our land, mountains, coal, watersheds and resources, so of course it's great for out-of-state corporations to come and exploit us.

One example of the exploitation of Appalachia for the benefit of the rest of the nation is the Kanawha Valley in West Virginia. The Kanawha Valley is the chemical production center for Union Carbide, DuPont, FMC, and other chemical corporations, and they use the valley to contain their chemical waste. Coincidently, the Kanawha valley has some of the highest cancer rates in the country. Appalachia gets the toxic residue, while the rest of the nation gets the product. The Appalachians have become America's toxic dumping ground.

A second example is Oak Ridge, Tennessee. It used to be a tiny Appalachian farming community called Wheat before the government seized the town and made it into a nuclear weapons production complex. Many people only had two weeks to evacuate their farms; they were told the checks for their loss were waiting for them at the Knoxville post office. During the manufacture of nuclear weapons, over half the world's mercury was used in that complex. Much of this mercury went down stream into the Clinch River, a tributary of the Tennessee River. As a result the Tennessee River has the highest heavy metal concentrations of any river on earth. And nearby Waits Bar Lake has detectable amounts of plutonium in the sediment.

Thanks to the Tennessee Valley Authority (TVA), the Appalachian Mountains also play host to the most ambitious nuclear power program in the nation—which means "cutting edge" 1970s nuclear plants and the barrels of toxic waste they produce. As with Oak Ridge, TVA's projects made Appalachian people refugees in their own country.

The question is—why is this acceptable? Why is Appalachia America's dumping ground?

Perhaps it has something to do with the mischaracterization of Appalachian history and people.

Real Appalachian history is largely ignored by the mass media, but it also might be the greatest tool we have to fight this misrepresentation of our people and region. The reality is that Appalachia has a long and proud history of political thought, resistance to power, art, craft, discourse, and music that is not accurately portrayed by the mass media. The people of Appalachia have contributed to the cultural and economic life of America to a degree few other regions can rival—but those contributions are not what come to the average American's mind when they think of us.

Appalachia has a rich history of resistance to arbitrary power and injustice. This region was instrumental in the abolitionist movement, and played a large part in the Underground Railroad. We can also look to the bloody, exploitative history of the coal industry to see brave examples of resistance to power and self-organization in the people of Appalachia. The coal miners of Appalachia were some of the first to strike and demand humane living conditions. Direct action and organizing models from the grassroots union organizing in Appalachia continue to influence the tactics used by other grassroots movements in America today.

We must combat the relegation of Appalachia to fourth world status. As long as the images and stereotypes are allowed to run unchecked, corporations and government agencies will continue to destroy our watersheds, mountains, and forests. The Appalachian Mountains are among the most diverse and lovely on Earth. They deserve better than complete destruction for the profit of a few. By embracing our true history, we will be better equipped to fight for a better future.

photo by Delilah O'Haynes

Erosion After Clear-Cut Logging

4:20 Poetry

by Jimbo

from Coal River Mountain Watch
Winter *Newsletter*, 2007

Four Twenty. It means many things
To many different folks
For some it's Hitler's Birthday
Or a day to smoke some dope

For me it holds a different meaning.
It's a certain time of day
I look Southwest and hold my Breath
As the mountains blown away

The ground beneath me trembles
As the sound like thunder rumbles past
The dust and ash rise skyward
Above the mighty blast

Machines descend into the rubble
Dozers, Loaders and Rock Drills
To labor through the dark of night
To shove rock into the hollers, what they call valley fills.

Each day the ridge line's smaller
Cause the machines they seldom stop
Except of course for shift change
Or their fuel tanks needing topped

One Day Peace will return here
When there's not more coal to dig
There will be just rubble
Where mountain once were big

Just scars where once was beauty
Streambeds of silt and sludge and more
What once was West Virginia
Will become a real eye sore

So just sit back and do nothing
Just like they tell you to!
And watch the mountains pass away
To make rich the chosen few

Although they do not live here
They know what's best for us
They tell us each and every day
In their judgment we must trust

So each day at 4:20
These thoughts pass through my head
I just hope it all ends soon
Before the Mountain's dead

I leave you now, with one more thought
Bring back the pick and shovel
If you can, put forth a plan
To stop Mountain Top Removal.

Mountain Truth

by Janet Keating

Ancestral mountains.
Keepers of eternal Truth—
Steep, hard-rock truth.
Pre-dawn woodthrush, echoing
down-in-the-valley truth;
Perennial streams cascading,
clear-running may-fly, caddis fly truth.
Wild ginger-covered hillside truth;
Wild, wild, wild winged truth.
Tree-nesting, ground-nesting cerulean and
black and white warbler truth;
Moth wings and pink lady slipper truth.
Water strew and fox squirrel truth;
Rich, dark sweet-smelling soft under each footfall
top-soil truth.
This soul. This soul. This wretched, lonely, God-longing soul
seeks and finds in these untamed mountains
Truth.

Almost Heaven, Not Almost Flattened

by Lauren Lambert

"Almost Heaven, West Virginia: Blue Ridge Mountains, Shenandoah River."

We all know this famous opening line of the John Denver song, "Country Roads." John Denver wrote this beloved song after being moved by the beauty of the mountains of West Virginia. And he had every right to write it. If you have ever seen a variety of pictures of the West Virginia Mountains, you have seen a natural beauty beyond compare. At one point in time, I would have wished this song our state song. However, with recent events, I think making this song our state song would be a disgrace to John Denver, and a mockery of the horrible happenings in our state. This travesty is referred to as mountaintop removal. By Webster's definitions, the word mountaintop means "summit, top of a mountain." The word removal means "the act of removing." Put these two definitions together, and you have "the act of removing a summit, top of a mountain." This is exactly what mountaintop removal is. Mountaintop Removal is "the most ruthless method yet found to extract coal as quickly and as cheaply as possible" (Reece, Appalachian Apocalypse). It is the coal company's new game to play with the low-sulfur, bituminous coal hiding in the tops of mountains all over the Appalachians, especially in West Virginia and Kentucky. This "cost efficient" way to extract coal is marring our "Almost Heaven." If we don't do something fast to fix this problem, the words will have to be changed to "Almost Flattened, West Virginia: Blown up mountains, sludge-filled river valleys." I feel that mountaintop removal is a problem harboring serious physical health risks, damaging psychological dangers, and a serious risk to the environment and should be completely eradicated, despite the seemingly positive light that the coal companies try to shed on it.

Mountaintop removal poses many physical health risks that the coal companies do not want you to know about, nor do they care whether or not you know about them. One of the major health concerns faced not only by the people of Appalachia but also all of America is the amount of mercury and carbon dioxide emissions released by mountaintop removal. It is as though Americans are "[paying] for the electricity with their health" (Sturr & Offner). Not only is the air polluted by this process but also "toxic heavy metals such as mercury, arsenic, copper, lead, and selenium are drained into headwaters that run all the way to the Gulf of Mexico" (Wellington, Strip Mining on Steroids). Focusing on the very real and immediate physical dangers to the people of Appalachia, according to an article by Beth Wellington, there is an elementary school in Marsh Fork sitting 400 yards from and directly in the path of nearly three billion gallons of coal slurry sludge. This is twenty times the amount of muck held back by the Buffalo Creek Dam that ruptured in 1972, killing 125 people (Wellington). There are nearly 500 of these "valley fillers," as the coal companies like to lightly put them, in the Appalachians. Each one is just like "a time bomb waiting to happen," states a Kentucky attorney (Mitchell). To me, however, these structures are "valley killers." Having the largest man-made earthen structure in America right in your state would seem like something to brag about. Well, it's not when that structure is the lifeless, moonscape slurry impoundment sitting on top of the headwaters of thousands of streams all across the state.

You may be wondering how in the world the proponents of mountaintop removal could look past these facts. Well, our coal is ultimately stolen from us by the tyrants of TNT. Our coal is taken everywhere, all over the country to be distributed and used for electricity, leaving behind ruins of death. Death of the mountains, death of a way of life, and possibly death of our people by the hazardous toxins left all over this poor state. Since we are "poor" though, we don't have much muscle behind us and people can easily look the other way when we "hillbillies" come looking for help to fight these corporate monsters. They seem to think that we don't know what is best for us, and that it is selfish for us to not want the mountaintops removed just because they "look pretty." They don't understand that it's not that we think that it just "looks pretty." When they take a piece of the land, they are taking a piece of the people as well, leaving a lifeless community.

Speaking of lifeless, the damage that this type of mining does to the people mentally is means for "[stopping] the madness" immediately ("Mountaintop Removal Fact Sheet"). The coal companies are ultimately running the people out of their towns in fear for their lives, like a bad outlaw would do in the old westerns. The people don't want to leave, nor should they have to. Some of these families have been rooted in these humble towns for generations. This rooting and sense of home, for some, is the only feeling of family they have left. To have to leave would make one feel lifeless. Stripping people of their homes is just as wrong as stripping the mountains of their summits. The coal companies have no right to do either. One man, Larry Gibson, had to face the remains of his family cemetery beaten down by a bulldozer that was driven carelessly over the headstones:

photo by Kayla Ward

Appalachian Vista

"What happened to the graves down here?" The man asks. "There were three graves over here and one over here." Larry Gibson has the desperate sound of a man who has just realized a terrible loss. "The people who are buried over there—or who were buried over there—are my great-great-great-grandparents," Gibson says, his voice choking. "It's my history they're wiping out—200 years of my past (Kovarik).

The fact is that there are too many instances of this sort taking place in the Appalachian region. It makes you stop and wonder what the coal companies are holding valuable. It is definitely not humankind or their emotions, which is a very sad and sorry thing to have to say. The companies even admit that "the only way [they] can turn a profit is to eliminate the workers—and that is what mountaintop removal [does.] These operations employ just 2,000 people" (Sturr & Offner). It is sad that the most lucrative business in the state and its way of life has become so distanced from its people that it is no longer about creating or keeping jobs for people, it is just about the money.

Not only are the coal companies not valuing humankind's emotions but also they are not valuing the environment which provides us with life and a way of life. "In West Virginia alone, [mountaintop removal] has destroyed more than 300,000 acres and buried over 1,200 miles of headwater streams" (Kovarik). These are streams that provide fish and other stream-dwellers a place to live, eat, grow, reproduce, animals with food to eat and water to drink, and food, recreation, and water for humans. The waters that the coal companies are destroying with their slurry slopes may seem like they are insignificant, but the companies are blind to the truth of the matter. "Today, not only can companies legally destroy wetlands and streams, but the Bush administration's new permitting procedures allow them to do so with no public notice and minimal review by federal authorities" (Sturr & Offner). And what about the mountaintops they are removing? These are homes to "more than 60 species of tree, which are in turn home to more than 250 different songbirds" (Reece). These birds are slowly but surely being wiped out of this region. Not only do the trees offer home for a wide variety of songbirds but also provide a home for all the animals that may live in a forest habitat. Squirrels, raccoons, bears, deer, coyotes, foxes, and so many more make their homes nestled within the forests. No wonder we have these animals moving in and rummaging through our garbage or killing our pets; we are tearing down their homes. Before we know it, the damaged land will be up to 1.4 million acres. Yes, "there will soon be enough flattened mountaintops in Appalachia— 1.4 million acres—to set down the state of Delaware on former summits" (Reece). This is having an effect on the environment that the coal companies don't want to believe in. There are two sad facts: One of the most "biologically diverse" habitats is being destroyed right before our very eyes for no other reason than to get to coal cheaply and quickly. The other sad fact is that if we continue to produce coal at this rate "by the industry's own estimates, West Virginia's coal may be gone in as few as 26 years" (Sturr & Offner). This is a very scary thought for me because if this is true, I will live to see a day when the second largest coal producing state is out of business.

This is the last thing on the company's minds though. All they want right now is to make a profit, no matter how damaging and lasting the effects are. "Of course, when coal companies publicly promote these techniques, they don't say that they're desperate to cut costs and are willing to wreck the environment to do it" (Sturr & Offner). They try to get the people off of their backs by saying that they will reclaim these sites they have so heartlessly destroyed. But it is just for that purpose: to get the people off of their backs. Rick Eades, after extensive research, claims that it will take "3,700 years to develop the rest of the permitted mountaintop removal sites." Now that one, sadly, isn't something I will live to see. If you think about it, by the time that would happen (if the companies would actually go through with their promises,) the generation living at that time would not even have the heart for these mountains that we have because the mountains will have been long gone.

Mountaintop Removal in Southern West Virginia

So, are you ready to imagine a world without our beloved mountain range? I know I am certainly not! The Appalachians are my home, my reason to stay here, and my reason to raise a family here, no matter what the cost. Having workers who come in and treat this land as if it is theirs to do with as they please is gut wrenching. Our love of the mountains should drive us to make sure that our neighbors are not continued to be tortured physically and mentally, and it should drive us to make sure that our way of life, supported by the environment, is no longer disrupted. The coal companies have decapitated one too many mountains, and it's high time that we do something to preserve our mountains. Yes, our mountains. They don't belong to a coal company; they belong to those who love them. Don't you protect what you love? We should take this quote by Larry Gibson into account: I say to you, and to you, what do you hold so precious in your own circle of life that you don't' have a price on it? What would it be? For me, it's Appalachia. For me, it's the mountains. For me, it's a whole way of life that they're wiping out here, and nobody seems to care!" (Kovarik).

If you care, you should do something about it. Get involved. Join an anti-MTR organization such as OVEC or ilovemountains.org. You definitely won't be sorry, and maybe one day, 3,700 years from now, your posterity won't have to imagine to understand the real lyrics of John Denver's beloved song with the famous starting line: "Almost Heaven, West Virginia. Blue Ridge Mountains, Shenandoah River."

Works cited —

Kovarik, Bill. "Stone's Throw." 22.3(2007): 48. InfoTrac. *Earth Island Journal.* Concord University Library. 12 Nov. 2007. <http://www.galegroup.com>

Mitchell, John G. "When Mountains Move." *National Geographic.* Mar 2006.

"Mountaintop Removal Fact Sheet." Ohio Valley Environmental Coalition. 08 Sep 2002. <http://www.ohvec.org/issues/mountaintop_removal/articles/2002_09_08.html>.

Reece, Erik. "Appalachian Apocalypse; Mountaintop removal: a ruthless method to extract coal as quickly and cheaply as possible.." 9.2(2007): 22. *On Earth*. InfoTrac. Concord University Library. 12 Nov. 2007. <http://www.galegroup.com>

Sturr, Chris and Amy Offner. "Flattening Appalachia." *Dollars & Sense* Issue 248(2003) 10-11. InfoTrac. Concord University Library. 12 Nov. 2007 <http://www.galegroup.com>

Wellington, Beth. "Extras—Commentary: Mountaintop Removal Sites—"Strip Mining on Steroids"." *llrx.com*. 22 Nov 2006. 20 Nov 2007 <http://www.llrx.com>

photo by Bob Gates

Mountaintop Removal Mining

Valleys Dammed

by p.j. laska

Valleys dammed
steep slopes logged,
coal gouged out
and trucked away

It looks like a sound
return on investment
with no other
price to pay.

Until the rains come
and the dammed up
impoundments
give way.

A raging wall
of water, rocks
and trees flattens
everything in its path.

Houses gone, roads
bridges. Those who
fled in fear come back
to a grim aftermath.

In flaying a mountain
to smoke the heart,
the whole is sacrificed
to the part.

There is no way
to reckon the loss
without tracing

addiction's cost.

Tour of Kayford Mountain—
October 16, 2006

by Jeff Mann

>   *for Edwina Pendarvis and Katie Fallon*

Today's quiet is arranged for us, the tourists of evisceration.
None of the usual dynamite, none of the usual

draglines gnawing innards like hagfish or lamprey.
It's an abeyance too large to fill

with words, though I try, naming plants
growing still in the face of blasphemy, mere

inches from the edge. I hug Eddy,
whisper *lamb's quarter, lady's thumb,*

motherfuckers, motherfuckers.
In what was heart and now is hole, air mounts

and hardens, dust swirls and settles, the felled
trees smoulder, a useless fuel. *Wild*

strawberry, dewberry, pokeweed. Crows circle
where the planet's darkness once was

dense, is now dispersed, in the emptiness left inside
when entrails are uncoiled and minced into bits.

Far below, a few trucks grumble with inertia,
sun shudders in the pit's black pools,

on the shattered shale. Here the forest ends,
the long drop begins. Here cedar waxwings

turn back. *Sumac's red, sugar maple's burn.*
Our weakness disappoints the dead. Here,

in the shiver of lavender asters, their faces appear,
their mute lips move. Glowering, they dissolve.

photo by Vivian Stockman

Mountaintop Removal Mining in West Virginia

Note from the publisher:

By now you may be growing weary of all the photographs of mountaintop removal devastation in this book. But that's how it is when one flies over the region—the destruction seems to go on and on forever. By 2012 an area of the Appalachians *twice the size of Rhode Island* will have been stripped.

Three Crosses

by Jeff Mann

> *for Cynthia Burack*

Isn't the ironweed enough?
And the hemlock needles edged with frost,
as if a castle's crenellations were carved from crystal?

To remind us of God's glory,
he said, and squandered a fortune on crosses,
trios blue and gold, making Calvary common as the next pasture,

the next interstate curve.
Isn't the Storm Moon enough, white pine boughs
shaking off snow? Crocus resurrection, purple and gold?

    *

This is what you do,
with your fat book of black and gold,
your love of mirrors, your stained-glass abbatoirs.

He hung on that prairie fence
for hours. She hanged herself in the barn.
His body was found in a toilet. She ran away from home.

This is what you do,
your prayers muttered in the voter's booth,
your certainty that a soiled world is soon due to end with you.

    *

Evil sees evil
everywhere. And so the streams run
orange, mountaintops peel off like scabs, red spruce needles

dissolve beneath sulfuric drizzle.
Evil only loves its own reflection, in broken
glass, in slurry puddles. Evil only loves what is eternal.

    *

What I want's a savior
in my sheets, brief as that bliss might be.
Brown eyes, brown goatee, thunderheads of body hair.

Some scruffy Christ
roped down, ball-gagged and melodic, eager as any sacrifice
to be eaten. What I want's a mountain landscape without a wound.

What I want's the skill
to break the jaw of vicious piety, the strength
to rescue what I love. What I want's a chainsaw on Easter Sunday,

and a heap of broken crosses
for the Beltane bonfire. My new world's the ring-dance,
the blaze, wine scented with woodruff, benediction of maple leaves.

Grandpa's Place

by Sam L. Martin

Where will I guide my
grandson to teach him to camp,
fish and hunt? I can
only tell stories
of my childhood, the mountains
and why God made them.
"Where that mountain used
to be," I will tell him, "my
buddies and I built
a lean-to and slept
under it three nights. When a
storm came, we got wet.
But that mountain's gone
with many other mountains."
I'm glad my grandpa
isn't here. There is
no place for his memories
to sleep and touch rain.

photo by Kent Kessinger

Appalachian Solitude

Ode to the Mountans

by Debra May-Starr

Help! My mountains are dying,
here in the West Virginia Hills.
Can you hear their moans and sighing,
as each branch of nature is killed?

Oh the trees are quietly weeping,
as the streams are quickly filled.
In our wells the poison is seeping,
even as the sun sets in it golden guild.

The fate of the nation has come to depend,
on the corporations and their dividends.
Logging, stripping, drilling—mines;
everybody's worried about that bottom line

Still she stands in all her glory,
that majestic mountain oh so high
and mother nature is imploring
for anyone—to help her dying mountains.

My Family in West Virginia, and How MTR Changed It

by Whitney Miller (age 12)

Hello, I am Whitney Miller and my family in West Virginia has lived with the coal mining for several years. Each year, me and my family go camping at the old house at Mud River. Before we had a campground at Berry's Branch, but we had to leave because of the coal mines.

Now our campsite at Mud River is not as much fun because of the coal mining. Before the coal mining came to our campground there were beautiful mountains and rivers. Me and my cousins always played in the river catching crawdads and fish, and we played on a big area of land. We played soccer, football, paintball guns, tackling, and lots of things. We would go back in the mountains and walk around. It was so much fun.

Now there is a big pond that destroyed the river, field and the mountains. The pond is very beautiful, with very deadly poisons in it. No one can swim, lay, live or anything because it's filled with poisons and chemicals. At night at our campsite all we hear is loud trucks moving back and fourth on the mountains; they are very noisy.

We are not allowed to go back to the mountains; they are destroyed because of the coal mining. The work that the coal mining has done is very ugly. It's horrible to look at. They have destroyed what West Virginia is known for . . . its mountains. When they destroyed these mountains they tore down trees and habitats. The animals that lived there have no home now.

Eventually, there will be no more places to camp in West Virginia. In my eyes, as a kid, the coal mining progress is shameful. I can't bear to look at what they have done to beautiful West Virginia.

When I go to West Virginia, I love to look at the mountains, but now when I look at them all I see is disaster. When I go to West Virginia I would love to see the mountains and be able to have adventures in them.

My great grandparents had to move out of their home because the coal company wanted them out of the way. They said no until they couldn't take the blasting that shook the house every day. My family also isn't happy with the coal company because of the Clean Water Act. That part of West Virginia gets their water from underground and then the coal company blasts the mountains, and it runs down into the water which they drink.

I wouldn't like it if I turned my water faucet on and black water came pouring out. My grandma and grandpa and I would always go four-wheeling on trails in the mountains. We would also go molly moocher hunting, picnicking, adventuring and more, but now we can't do as much because the mountains are disappearing.

I love West Virginia. It's my favorite place to be, and it always will be no matter what anyone does to it.

photo by Kent Kessinger

Swimming in the Appalachians

The Mourning Mountains

by an Anonymous Deer Hunter

After a 30-minute climb in the darkness, I stopped to rest a few minutes. It was 6:45 a.m., December 2, 2004. A deer blew at me about 75 yards on up the mountain; somewhere up in the oak timber, so I decided to wait for daylight right where I was.

As the pinkish glow in the east gave way to another day, I found myself unable to concentrate on scanning for deer, as the totally unnatural and ungodly view 600 yards to my left dominated my full attention. I was shocked and sickened.

The entire uppermost section of the left side of 4 mile Hollow—bordering the Kanawha State Forest, near Marmet, WV—was gone! The thousands of giant oak, hickory and beech trees, which stood there for the past century, had vanished forever.

Anger, then rage set in. One of the most beautiful, big-timbered, wildlife rich hollows in Kanawha County is now a mountaintop removal wasteland. And the world is expected to just accept this shock and awe campaign against the Appalachian Mountains.

Our state and federal regulatory agencies and our elected politicians just turn their heads and let them get by with this, in seeming homage to the coal industry's propaganda and deceptive slogans: I love Coal — Cleaner Greener Coal — Friends of Coal — Mountaintop Mining; It's the Right Thing to Do.

The vast majority of the rest of the educated world—many of whom were involved in the draft environmental impact study (EIS) on mountaintop removal—think it is simply The Wrong Thing To Do. The research confirmed that approximately 1,200 miles of mountain streams have already been buried forever with blasted "overburden" and over one million acres of the most supreme forest on Earth have already been or will be obliterated. Forever.

Polls have shown that the majority of West Virginians are opposed to mountaintop removal. So, why are we permanently annihilating the landscape of large portions of southern West Virginia, altering the aquatic systems of Mother Nature, creating ghost towns out of dozens of 150 year old communities, allowing a practice which, with its accompanying permanent forest mutilation, is the direct cause of the severity of all the recent ravaging floods in southern WV, and furthermore, impairing both the physical and mental well-being of human beings who live near mountaintop removal projects? (While promoting, of all things, tourism!)

The answer is so very simple. All of these atrocities against Earth and crimes against society are for the sake of a couple of multi-billion dollar corporations that mine coal using the absolute cheapest method possible, while employing the absolute fewest number of workers possible!

Yes, presently coal provides 52 percent of the electricity consumed in the United States. But, has government or industry ever conducted any research to determine if this 52 percent could still be feasibly produced with time-honored and respected underground mining, couple with more easily mined western coal? And how many more thousands of coal mining jobs would still be in West Virginia and Kentucky if mountaintop removal had not reared its ugly head?

Folks it's never been clearer: The Will of the People is being totally ignored because of the sickening greed of the owners and managers of large corporations, who immorally and unjustly pander their influence with policy makers.

When an industry that has approximately 3 percent of the total workforce of an entire state has the power to successfully appeal and unfairly overturn every ruling that federal judges have made against illegal mountaintop removal practitioners, then we have already entered a period in American history which one of our most famous and respected presidents warned about many decades ago: Franklin D. Roosevelt, who said, "The liberty of a democracy is not safe if the people tolerate the growth of private power to a point where it becomes stronger than their democratic state itself."

That brings to mind another famous and respected President's statement. Abraham Lincoln said, "and that Government, of the people, by the people, for the people, shall not perish from the Earth."

The Character of Mountains

by Delilah F. O'Haynes

People who built log and plank dwellings
on steep Appalachian hillsides became
the rugged mountains they clung to.

Coal mining gear, 1950s: a carbide lamp,
its pungent, stinging odor filling dank air;
dinner buckets loaded with egg salad sandwiches,
hot coffee, moon pies; flannel long-johns
and stiff coveralls—soaked in Tide, run
through the wringer and hung on the line
to freeze in January wind; steel-toed,
lace-up boots of worn, gritty-black leather.

Mine strike, Clinchfield Coal, Virginia, 1965:
men stood vigil through long, cold
nights, telling their stories over fires
built in oil barrels, fortifying courage
with strong coffee and moonshine.

Farmington, West Virginia, 1968:
78 men died in explosion at Consol
No. 9. Townspeople rallied
round miners, their families; Nixon
signed mine safety act, 1969.

A quarter-century later:
augers pierce Earth's skin, plunge
like daggers into mountainsides;
dynamite shatters landscapes,
decapitates mountains;
bulldozers strip away top soil,
hack mountains to stair-step ridges;
logging and dump trucks
haul away earth and trees.

Flood, West Virginia, McDowell, 2001:
Eight inches of rain—run-off carves
new streams through naked hillsides.
Gymnasium at Welch Middle School
buried under mountain of mud;

town of Mullens washed away;
whole families smothered
by mud in homes and vehicles.

Mountain ruins flank back roads
and interstates, unnoticed by passersby.

Poem originally published in *The Character of Mountains*,
a portion of the proceeds for this book donated to OVEC.

Rendering Appalachia

by Delilah F. O'Haynes

All things are connected like the blood that unites us. We did not weave the web of life. We are merely a strand in it. Whatever we do to the web, we do to ourselves.
—Chief Seattle, Suquamish, *1854*

My Daddy mined coal all his life, in Virginia, West Virginia, and Kentucky—before and after serving in World War II. As I describe him in my poem, "Portrait of a Coal Miner," Robert A. Hibbitts was "accustomed to speaking to stark white/eyeballs fixed in masks of coal dust./He can't remember breathing without/ the smell of sulfur or looking in the mirror/without raccoon eyes staring back" (lines 13-17). Daddy did strip mining, after he could no longer pass the physical exam to go down in the mine; but he made sure to work for a small, hometown company that went beyond laws of reclamation because he loved these hills.

My daddy *was* these mountains. When he wasn't working or sleeping, he roamed the hillsides—coon hunting, fishing, gathering ginseng, picking huckleberries, or just walking the land. He knew the importance of preserving medicinal plants like mullein, a Native American herb which grows abundantly in Appalachia; and he knew the necessity of keeping our streams and rivers clean. He often bragged that our mountain spring water was the clearest, cleanest water on earth. "Red," as Dad was known to his friends, was acquainted with every inch of the mountains that surrounded our hollow. He taught me to revere the wildness of the earth because it is sacred.

Daddy was a sergeant in the 77th Division of the Army in the war, stationed in the Pacific—the Philippine Islands and Okinawa. Those boys saw hell up close and brought a little of it back with them. Like many of those soldiers, he was plagued with nightmares of losing boys in his platoon, watching men being ripped apart or burned, and seeing piles of bodies on every island—even women and children.

At the end of the fighting, Dad flew over Japan and witnessed the destruction of Hiroshima. He never spoke of what he saw from the plane that day. But he came back to these Appalachian Mountains, named for the Apalachee Indians who first settled the Southern Appalachians, with a determination to make a safe home for his future wife and any children they might have. The only place he wanted to be was deep in the loving folds of the oldest mountain range on earth—among people as rugged as the mountains. Here was security. Here was peace.

Red bought a two-room log cabin on a rocky hillside surrounded by woods and streams, and there he raised his family and went to work in the mines for more than twenty years, never knowing that some day, the companies that put food on his table would come into these hills, armed with lethal ammonium nitrate and bulldozers, and level the very mountains that became his life and sustenance—just to remove the coal he worked so hard everyday to extract, coal that is easily burned and forgotten.

Chief Seattle said, "To harm the earth is to heap contempt on its Creator." He predicted that if we continued to desecrate the planet which sustains us, we would "one night suffocate in [our] own waste." Tonight in West Virginia, children sleep with their shoes on in case of sudden, toxic flooding, and some of these children wonder when their mother will succumb to the copper, mercury, and arsenic in her liver. If my Daddy were alive today, I know he would prefer to risk his own life down in the mine rather than have women and children threatened by defiled air and poisonous sludge dams that leach deadly metals and chemicals into our water supplies.

I'm glad Red isn't here now to witness the destruction I've seen up close. Gone are his wild huckleberries and much of his mountain ginseng. But I'm here to speak for him. When I look on the environmental devastation caused by mountaintop removal, especially the mountains that nourished and protected my childhood, and see its effects on humans—loss, displacement, death—I feel the heart within me ripped out and cast aside. I'm reminded of the words of Chief Seattle, and I know, just as my Daddy knew, that these mountains, these sacred lands, are life to us. What we do to these mountains, we do to ourselves.

Highland Whisper

by Delilah F. O'Haynes

I am piney woods,
cool of creek trickling
over mossy rocks.
I am mountain coal,
shining like black diamonds
washed up at river's edge,
dark beltway through
mountain's belly.
I am rush of waterfall,
crystal white life force
cascading over
ancient boulders.
I am hush of marshland,
oozing bog, delicate flowers,
fertile virgin earth
stretching reverently
toward crimson horizon.
I am highland ridges,
eagle heights that
brush azure skies,
unworn by winter winds.
I am rocky core
beneath creek bed,
pink laurel blossoms
peeking through piney woods.

Originally published in
The Character of Mountains, 2006

photo by Kent Kessinger

Appalachian Forest

Tennessee Dam Break:
Another Message for Clean Energy

by Delilah F. O'Haynes

Harriman, Tennessee, December 22, 2008: quaint suburban homes decorated for the holidays swam in hundreds of acres of gray, toxic mud. Thousands of fish lay belly-up along the shorelines of the Emory and Clinch Rivers. Tennessee Valley Authority (TVA) officials evacuated residents, avoiding the possible initial death toll that befell the Buffalo Creek community in West Virginia in 1972, when a sludge dam break took the lives of 125 people and injured over a thousand. TVA also blocked the two affected rivers, which flow into the Tennessee River, in an effort to avoid major arsenic contamination, but too late. Arsenic and other deadly toxins had already flowed as far south as Chattanooga.

Law suits by homeowners are pending. Environmentalists say the spill was avoidable. TVA says the spill was caused by the large amounts of rain that fell over a short amount of time in December. Residents say it was just a matter of time before such an environmental catastrophe occurred because many small spills had already occurred over the last few years. TVA says clean-up is underway and area water will be returned to safe drinking level standards as soon as possible. However, Americans are no longer distracted by such assurances. The Buffalo Creek community has never fully recovered from their disaster, even though law suits were settled, because officials never followed up on promises to rebuild the community.

The facts: TVA's Kingston Fossil Fuel Plant dike breach spilled more than five million cubic yards of fly ash over Roane County, Tennessee, spreading dangerous levels of arsenic, along with lead, mercury, and thallium, over an entire neighborhood and possibly affecting the rest of Tennessee's water supply. For years, the Environmental Protection Agency (EPA) has worked to hold back global warming by improving air quality with restrictions on power plants that use fossil fuels. But what about ground water quality affected by toxic fly ash? One solution to the problem of toxic fly ash waste has been to contain it within cement. However, do we want to build our homes, schools, and hospitals using cement blocks of toxic waste? No matter where toxic wastes are stored, the toxins are still on the planet. No method can make five million cubic yards of toxic fly ash disappear. There is no such thing as toxic waste clean-up.

America is the biggest contributor to global warming. Why would we consciously continue to rely on fossil fuels such as coal for energy when power plants run by fossil fuels, says the EPA, are the largest contributors to mercury contamination in our country?

photo courtesy Tennessee Mountain Defense

TVA Coal Ash Sludge Spill, Tennessee, 2008

According to Greg Haegele and Bruce Niles of the Sierra Club, an environmental group, nearly seventeen percent of American women already have enough mercury poisoning to negatively affect their future offspring. Mercury is just one of the deadly toxins produced by fossil-fuel consumption.

The TVA Kingston Fossil Fuel Plant was finished in 1955. The Industrial Revolution sparked an era of fossil-fuel use that escalated after World War II. But it also led to new technology that allows us to take advantage of clean, renewable energy. Many politicians now understand that America must become energy independent; to many Americans, this means using our own coal and oil deposits. Despite the politicians' rhetoric, there is no such thing as "clean coal." Although it may burn clean once it is harvested and processed, the harvesting process still leaves deadly toxins behind. Coal, say Haegle and Nilles of the Sierra Club, "is filthy, it is destructive when mined, it is poisonous when burned and it contaminates ground water when the coal ash is land-filled. Not so with investments in energy efficiency, wind, solar and geothermal power."

Along with pollution that contributes to global warming, extracting coal from the ground has another negative effect. Ironically, filthy coal left in its habitat has a natural purpose as a carbon filter for rainwater. It filters out the arsenic, mercury, and lead in the ground that would otherwise leach into our rivers and streams— that's what makes it so filthy. Harvested and burned, coal is gone for many thousands of years, and we are left without that natural water filter.

With new technology to harness the renewable powers of wind and sun, we can make the Twenty-First Century the era of clean energy and leave the remaining coal within the ground for its natural purpose. Now is the time to end fossil-fuel consumption, before another toxic sludge dam breaks.

Letters in the Daily Mail —

Ohio Valley Environmental Coalition Newsletter

Lorelei Scarbro: Mountaintop mining pollutes as it destroys

Mountaintop mining pollutes as it destroys

I, too, attended the hearing pertaining to the mountaintop removal site of Jupiter Holdings in Boone County. There was a wide age range represented in the courtroom on both sides.

The majority of the people who have been referred to as "retired environmentalists," to my knowledge, are still actively working and supporting their local economy.

There is a vast difference between erecting strategically placed buildings on a "reclaimed strip job" and a mountaintop removal-valley fill like the Mt. View School in McDowell County. This school crumbles a little more every day.

He who shall not be named has discovered the best way around the reclamation laws is to donate the valley fill to the local school board and the taxpayers get to pay for the reclamation.

My husband died of black lung after 35 years of union coal mining. I am not opposed to responsible mining. Everyone should have the right to support his family.

This fight for me is not about saving a tree or a mountain. If we poison our air and water, which is what mountaintop removal does, what do we have left?

Nothing else matters if you can't breathe.

—Rock Creek, WV

Melvin L. Tyree: We must save Earth for next generation

This letter is written in reference to the Oct. 14 letter, "Mining destroys God's mountains." Whether one chooses to believe Creation is God's gift to humanity or if Creation is a wondrous accident of nature, the present generation has a spiritual and moral obligation to preserve that gift for the generations that follow us.

This obligation to be proper stewards of Creation transcends tomorrow's paycheck, next week's mortgage or even next year's corporate profit returns for Big Coal's CEOs. It is in essence the world we leave our children.

Nothing is more important than that.

We are now seeing the impacts to their future. Our arctic ice cap is being threatened with irreversible melting due to the carbon dioxide we so foolishly emit into our atmosphere from burning billions of tons of coal and petroleum every year. If this practice continues for just another eight or 10 years, that ice cap will be destined for oblivion. And with it, Nature's fury will be unleashed upon the United States like nothing that has been seen since our species evolved.

If we are so stupid as to continue mining and burning coal like there is no tomorrow, no tomorrow is exactly what Nature will give us. Without that ice cap, ocean currents will change, prevailing weather patterns will shift and our arctic air will no longer be cooled from the natural radiator of the Arctic.

This is it. We must decide now if we're going to be "Friends of Coal" and go out in a crazed carbon-fueled blaze of glory, or dig our heels in, turn the ship into the wind and fight for the generations that follow us. —Hurricane, WV

Briana McElfish: Residents deserve better than coal

One recent weekend, I visited an awesome example of what our fossil fuel dependence costs us. At Kayford Mountain I saw not just the destruction of the mountains but heard from people whose health and livelihood are threatened every day by mountaintop removal coal mining.

Mingo County fought three years just to get drinkable water after theirs was poisoned in the industry's attempt to dispose of coal waste, and now communities across the state are facing the same plight, including a range of cancers, liver, kidney and reproductive diseases.

Residents in Boone County are subjected to so much coal dust that some who have never entered a mine suffer from black lung disease. I watched children play in the leaves and realized their young bodies are being exposed to the consequences of mountaintop removal pollution. They are West Virginia's future. They deserve so much better.

In order to end this devastation, we must end mountaintop removal and ensure a just transition for workers into a new clean energy economy so that West Virginia may prosper and our people may thrive. Conservation and renewable energy help more than just birds and trees; after all, who's dying for your cheap energy?
—Huntington, WV

Sludge or Slurry Pond

Counting Crosses

lyrics by T. Paige

Counting crosses under the moonlight
wondering Lord what does it mean
when they shove the mountains into the valley
with the crosses underneath

Can you hear those bulldozers comin'
Can you hear the big machines
getting closer every day
and we all know what it means

We will rise, we will rise
Now is the time and we will rise

Mountain people throughout the land
Now is the time to take your stand
Standing right beside you is an angel band
His holy mountains to defend

One sparrow falling one grain of sand
one drop of rain from the sky
He sees the mountains He knows their names
and He can hear a mountain cry

We will rise, we will rise
Now is the time and we will rise

Mountaintop Removal: An Outsider's View of a Growing National Tragedy

by Suzanne Rebert

People are always asking me why I moved here. That's not a question I heard much back in Seattle or even Salt Lake City where I grew up. It's true that I did graduate work on the economics of regulatory change in the Alaskan halibut fishery. No one has ever caught halibut in the Ohio River, and I wouldn't eat any if they did. It's also true that my original reason for moving 2,800 miles, to a state where I knew no one, has disappeared. In its place, however, I've found true friendships and a landscape with much to love about it. Trees, birds, rocks, foods, accents, churches, politics: everything is a little different.

Through my involvement here, I've had the chance to see an environmental travesty that boggles my mind—a real funhouse-mirror view of economic development. I appreciate this opportunity to share a newcomer's impressions of mountaintop removal.

On October 25, four of us from OVEC, as well as Larry Gibson, joined other activists, locals, attorneys and reporter Penny Loeb on a tour of mountaintop removal/valley fill sites in the coal-rich hills of Raleigh County.

This was my first visit to rural Appalachia. There was so much to see and think about. We drove along dirt roads, back into the "hollers," where twilight comes so early and shy children play in ill-fitting hand-me-downs and magnificent cocks strut in their pens. There were cows, horses, goats, chickens, hound dogs, and beehives; the trees—apple, walnut, beech, oak, maple, locust, sycamore, tulip-tree—gently rained colored leaves on the sodden earth, and thick vines draped the limbs.

There are pawpaws and persimmons here, too, and Appalachia is also where much of the world's ginseng comes from; the mountain people harvest it, and goldenseal and other medicinal herbs, for their own use as well as for sale. Frogs and salamanders, which are vanishing from so many of the world's ecosystems, have thrived here. We saw wild turkey tracks and black bear scat. Many of the houses and trailers were poor, yet they were gaily decorated for Halloween. There were small wooden churches everywhere, and old barns, and big pickups.

We stood at a bend in a road by pretty White Oak Creek, which swelled last spring from surface mining runoff and drowned a young mother and a neighbor boy who had left their stalled car on the way home from Wednesday night service. At the head of this creek and many others loom the mountaintop removal sites, where the hills are leveled by huge draglines after all the trees have been logged off. The coal is extracted and the overburden is then dumped into the ravines. Inadequate holding ponds are constructed behind rough earthen dams to hold the runoff. We passed blasting warning signs to see the fetid pond that had failed to protect the woman and boy. About 25 years ago, a dam like this gave way at Buffalo Creek, and 125 people were killed.

That incident led to the passage of SMCRA, which dictates that strip miners return the land to its original contours . . . "except. . . ." A loophole was carefully crafted to allow the wholesale rape of the land that's going on now.

When mountaintop removal mining is over, the mountains are flat and the hollers aren't hollow. Grasses and little shrubs are seeded over the acidic gravel that remains. If the reclamation contractor goes bankrupt after the coal company has moved on, nothing is seeded over anything.

I've been to Mount St. Helens. Volcanoes are Nature's way of recycling rock subducted at the boundaries of tectonic plates. They are places of awesome destruction and creativity. The new land becomes fertile' we owe agriculture, metals, and probably the existence of large oceans to this violent process.

Much that I saw that Saturday bore a superficial resemblance to the area near Mount St. Helens.

But instead of recycling rock, water and minerals, the companies are extracting short-term revenues and redistributing them away from the people who are left to deal with the costs. The industry has laid off thousands of miners as it has become more capital-intensive, yet the patterns of dependence and fear remain. Things happen to local people who speak out against the abuse of SMCRA and the destruction of their homes. The West Virginia and Kentucky legislatures feed on coal money.

This is low-sulfur coal, too; and don't you use electricity like everyone else? There's a problem, though, I expect to pay for electricity with money. Not with people's lives, and not with the destruction of the earth.

As a natural resource economist I'm interested in the way local communities can love and sustain the environment that supports them. This respectful relationship is founded on knowledge gleaned from generations of experience; it has been observed among Aleut sea lion hunters, East African herdsmen, and others.

Close-knit communities that "do good science" (understand the environment they use) and accept the costs as well as the benefits of the harvest, can actually regulate themselves. Give the costs to some people and the benefits to others, and you have environmental abuse and social injustice. It had happened and continues to happen in the coal fields of Appalachia.

It needs to stop. There is too much beauty and knowledge and life at stake here. And ultimately, we all live down stream.

photo by Delilah O'Haynes

Clean Coal Comes to Virginia

Through the Eyes of a Child

by Tashina Savilla

Imagine that as a child you often visited a favorite picnic spot, set on a mountain. Beautiful mountains and endless forests surrounded you, as far as you could see. The cool, crisp smell of the fresh mountain air soothed your lungs as you breathed. It was as close to heaven as you would ever get in your whole life.

Now imagine going back to that same spot, as an adult, but instead of the wilderness, you only saw bare mountaintops, stripped of their beauty by mining companies.

There are several ways in which mining can be safe and environmentally effective. For instance, deep mining doesn't destroy the surface of the mountains as much, but mining companies don't want to spend that much money when they can save a few bucks and completely destroy West Virginia's mountains.

Mountaintop removal and valley fills will forever be a curse to West Virginia's beautiful mountains, unless we can do something to save them. Our mountains are too precious and our wildlife too significant to just let them slip away without a fight. Once they are gone, it will never be the same, no matter how much the companies reclaim.

The simple insignificance of money can never take the place of this. It is the profit motive and, too often, greed, that has cursed West Virginia's mountains. Coal mining has destroyed too much of every Mountaineer's principal blessing: our majestic mountains. Our mountains can't take much more.

Tashina is a high school student who lives on Cabin Creek,
in the heart of massive mountaintop removals and valley fills.

An Open Letter to W.V. Governor Joe Manchin

August 25, 2006

Dear Governor Manchin:

West Virginia's dirty coal secret is spilling out faster than a sludge dam failure. It's out beyond the state's borders. It's out through excellent magazine features on the national and international level. It's out because of the efforts of informed and dedicated members of state, regional and national environmental groups.

It's out because of brave individuals who have taken action after their state and federal officials have hidden in the pockets of the coal barons for better than a century, allowing these exploiters to destroy the land, the culture, the health and the spirit of hundreds of thousands of people.

This past April, I spent most of a day on Blair Mountain. Part of this extensive topography has been forever desecrated by mountaintop removal mining. However, much of it remains relatively pristine, with clean cool streams, flowing through hardwood forests. I was fortunate enough to photograph some of these latter scenes. How long will they remain this way? I also photographed an Arch Coal site that has been closed since 1999. After seven years, it has nothing but non-native grass.

A mountaintop removal site on Cazy Mountain, in Boone County, was "reclaimed" 22 years ago. It sprouts nothing but non-native grass, and a few thin, nasty-looking, non-native shrubs. Where is the earth-cooling hardwood forest? Where is the native ginseng that mountaineers have always been able to dig to sell and use? Where are the deer, the turkeys, the many species of songbirds, small mammals and other animals? Where are the clean, swift-flowing streams and their native trout? Where is life-giving soil? Where is life?

During my weeklong stay, I photographed and witnessed enough to know that everything I'd read and heard about the problems in this region is worse when viewed up close. Add to all the other woes caused by mountaintop removal mining the visibly-obvious fact that these sites help increase global warming.

You may know that Pennsylvania, which has contributed much coal to this nation, and much coal-related pollution and human misery, now generates more wind power than any other state east of the Mississippi. That's only the beginning. Pennsylvania is upping the ante with wind power, placing a facility in the coal country of Cambria County. Residents will be able to continue their legacy of providing energy, but now this will be clean energy. It won't kill and maim workers by explosion, by mine collapse, by black lung. It won't foul our streams or contribute to acid rain, or to mercury poisoning. It won't require that people mow down forests, and blow up mountains which have stood for millions of years. Wind and solar power will be a ticket to freedom, to real social and economic progress and promise.

But what about West Virginia, which has the opportunity to do much the same? The state over which you preside as chief executive, is now treating potential wind generation projects as the enemy, or something that needs more study. How dare you allow the suffocation of progress.

Are wind farms especially scenic? No, but they are visions of hope. Do they cripple thousands of workers, spew toxic waste into the air and water? No. Do they destroy the health and culture of the residents? No. Can they be dismantled and the sites returned to their natural states if better energy technology comes along? They certainly can.

Last year, our photography business took us to Tuscany, Italy. In one area, we noticed a network of pipes and related hardware stretching out near ground level. The odor of sulfur was evident. Our friends informed us that this system transports geothermal energy from hot springs in the region; that the steam derived from the earth helps generate enough electricity to completely power some small towns in the area.

Was the system pretty? Not especially. Is mountaintop removal pretty? Is a coal treatment facility or a coal-fired power plant pretty? I think you know the answers. Do the benefits of geothermal power and wind power outweigh the inconveniences? Can the benefits of any kind of coal mining, especially mountaintop removal, barely approach the misery and the environmental, health and economic plight they cause? You know those answers, too.

In southern West Virginia and eastern Kentucky, descendants of the proudest, most independent and most patriotic of all American populations are now slaves in their own land. They are victims of true terrorism committed by American corporations on American soil, with the blessing of their own governments. Residents outside the coal fields are learning that basic human rights are being violated wholesale in your state. When individuals stand up for what is right, and are repaid by physical threats and vandalism, their vehicles tampered with, their pets killed; when their land, and their water are poisoned, and corporate officials can dismiss these floods as "acts of God," and can get away with it; when long-time residents are forced off their land, and their health sacrificed on the altar of short-term profit, that's human rights abuse; that's terrorism.

But, as I said governor, the secret is out, and Massey can't put it back. Arch Coal and all the other companies that have raped the land and the people of the southern Appalachians for a century, can't put it back. People in Pennsylvania are getting the story. People in California, in Nebraska, in England, all over Europe and the rest of the world are getting the story.

Since no one can shove the secret back into it's dirty bag, you have an opportunity to do what's right for your fellow West Virginians-- the ones who are bravely doing what is right, the ones who are yet afraid to stand up, for fear of economic and physical retribution, the ones who don't know how free people take charge of their lives, and the ones yet to be born. You can do what's right and help abolish mountaintop removal mining.

We all know that coal mining, especially mountaintop removal mining, is not about providing energy, or any such patriotic-sounding smokescreen. It's about sociopaths going where the laws are lax, non-existent or poorly-enforced, because lax laws and non-enforcement of decent laws allow these exploiters to make immense sums of money, and pass on the real environmental, social and financial cost of coal mining to the public. We also know that much of the coal mining companies' land and mineral rights were obtained through deception, and worse. And, regardless of how they obtained those "rights," they have no right to commit wholesale destruction of mountains, forests, streams, human health and spirit.

Theodore Roosevelt probably said it best. "Every man holds his property subject to the general right of the community to regulate its use to whatever degree the public welfare may require it."

A former professor of well-known photographer Larry Ulrich also observed, "If you don't believe in nature as a divine force, you won't go to hell, you live in one."

Governor Manchin, on this issue, you can either work for the people, or you can be in the hands of the coal companies. You cannot have it both ways. I believe you can do the right thing. If it costs you your job, you'll still have done the right thing. Your courage will open new doors. You'll be able to look at these photographs, and into the eyes of your fellow West Virginians, and sleep well. The damage that has been done and is being done will last for thousands of years, and through hundreds of generations. All of those generations will look back on what has been done in the past thirty years and say, "Who could have let this happen?" Please don't be one of those who lets this happen. Don't let them blame it on God. Do you think that God would create something as beautiful and as loving as the mountains and forests of West Virginia, and destroy them and the people who have lived as one with the land? You know the answer.

Thank you.

Mark Schmerling

Mountain Air

by Marlene Simpson

Praise the Lord from the earth, . . .Fire, and hail; snow, and vapours; stormy wind fulfilling His word; Mountains, and all hills; fruitful trees, and all cedars:
                    —Psalms 148:7-9 KJ

Mountain Air, intoxicating,
Breathed in deeply walking—waiting.

Your blest scents defy describing,
My nostrils thrill to their imbibing.

Each tree offers a fragrance fine,
Like sweet bouquet from vintage wine.

Mountain Air, you tease my senses,
Relax my guard and my defenses.

Mountain Air, you calm my soul,
With gentle ease disarm control.

Mountain Air, the breath of God
Breathed on me my heard to prod,

Rekindling fires of thanks and praise,
For Mountain walks on mountain ways.

The Heart of Me

by Marlene Simpson

Come, I'm a wellspring living and free,
Flowing o'er the brim in the very heart of me.

I'm iris, stately and morning dew kissed
By glistening droplets from low-hanging mist.

I'm pink morning glories and fragrant honeysuckle vines
Gracing fence rows and cornstalks I don and entwine.

I'm radiant diamonds—mountain settings enfolded in white,
The Jeweler's dazzle at dawning, His winter's yawn in the night.

I'm shady hike trails and churning white waters;
I'm solitude and thrills my dear sons and daughters.

I'm ever changing hues in the morning sunrise,
And blazing sunsets adorning twilight skies.

I'm cascading falls and meandering streams,
The subjects of poets, and artists, and dreams.

I'm black bear, wild turkey, and white tail deer,
You might chance to see should I chance appear.

I'm coyotes and foxes roaming knob land and field,
Searching for prey, which perhaps they may yield.

I'm barn swallows swooping the freshly cut fields
To catch insects the mower stirs, for opportune meals.

I'm a cow defying gravity grazing steep grassy hills
And amazing passersby with my balancing skills.

I'm wooly worms, walnuts and high mountain fogs,
Lightning bugs, crickets, and green peeping frogs.

I'm apple butter simmering; I often draw a gathering.
Stir and sniff, dream of the baked goods I'll be slathering.

I'm soup beans and cornbread, grits, country ham,
Fried green tomatoes, collard greens, and fried spam.

I'm bluegrass music in an ole country store,
Antique and craft shops you'll love to explore.

I'm a special afternoon hot air balloon race,
Or a roam on the Roan with butterflies to chase.

I'm old airy barns where tobacco leaves hang,
On days when the wind gusts my loosened doors bang.

I'm chimney smoke swirling when fire is stoked,
When cool, damp, night air falls, I hang like a cloak.

I'm swings out on porches or old back yard trees
For oldsters and youngsters to swing in the breeze.

I'm a one room school house of memories way back,
Potbelly stoves, ink wells and lunch in a sack.

I'm quaint country churches where Jesus is preached
For the tempted, the tossed, and the lost to be reached.

I'm a farmer, worker of the soil, tending crops to reap
Trusting God for growing rains and rest so I can sleep.

I'm men in bibs throwing horseshoes, playing checkers,
Courting sweeties with flowers and ice cream double-deckers.

I'm old gents on liars' benches swapping our views
And we know they work 'cause we've paid our dues.

I'm a woman, a lady, who will follow, who will lead;
I help those who grace my life with wisdom, word and deed.

I'm brave volunteers, still answering the call,
Who will fight for liberty and justice for all.

I'm storytelling, rich history, and melodious tale,
A cool satisfying drink for thirsty souls to avail.

I am what I am, Appalachian and free
Come, I'm the heart of East Tennessee.

A Right to have Rights

by Juanita Sneeuwjagt
Committee for Constitutional and Environmental Justice

My story began while hiking over my land on Backbone Ridge, in Dickenson County, Virginia, during the summer of 2006. I was amazed to find bright pink ribbons tied around several trees with their tails blowing in the breeze. It appeared someone (ones) had been trespassing and surveying on my land without my knowledge or consent. A nearby neighbor said she saw men surveying and thought they were employed by me.

Later that year in November 2006, I received a phone call. The caller identified himself as Gabriel Rasnick employed with Equitable Gas Production located at that time at Big Stone Gap, VA, with the home office being in Pennsylvania via West Virginia.

After much verbal bantering the caller said, "Equitable wants a land lease" on my land on Backbone Ridge. I asked for what purpose. He said Equitable wanted to explore gas well drilling, laying of pipelines, situating holding tanks, and building rights of way and any other thing Equitable was desirous of doing. He said Equitable was willing to give me **$5.00 per acre** in exchange for the land lease. I told him absolutely NO!

After consulting with my siblings, they all said "NO" to a land lease or any kind of lease granted to Equitable Gas or any of their affiliates. At that time I sent to Equitable a letter and a map to clarify the land that was not to be trespassed upon. The letter stated that at no time may Equitable or anyone, for any reason, trespass upon our land. Mr. Don Hall, Equitable's "Land Man" signed the green card certifying that he had received it and the post office returned it to me.

As the months went by Equitable Gas Company again attempted to reach my eleven siblings, who also said NO! again to the granting of a land lease. The understanding being that if one sibling said "YES" to a land lease, that yes constituted the agreement of all twelve siblings to a land lease.

In June of 2007, I received a call that the Virginia Gas and Oil Board was to meet in Abingdon, VA. The board's function is to regulate the activities of the various gas companies in Southwest Virginia and hold them in compliance with the rules governing the activities of the gas companies.

I raced up from North Carolina to attend the June meeting of the VA Gas and Oil Board. The various gas companies along with Equitable were present along with their attorneys and sometimes their surveyors and engineers and their "land men," men who appear to have the job of attaining rights of way by whatever method possible.

I was allowed to testify (no small feat, since there are strict criteria as to regulations to testify). I testified strongly, saying I was not aware of the Virginia Law (Code) saying that the "Natural and coal bed methane gas under the ground now belonged to the Commonwealth of Virginia." Also I wished to consult an attorney who would acquaint me of my legal rights. The VA gas and Oil Board granted me one month to collect the information I needed.

During the following month I contacted local attorneys. None would help me. I called the VA Attorney Referral Service. They could not recommend even one attorney who could help me!! I contacted attorneys all the way to Richmond, VA. None would help me. For the most part they were already retained by the gas companies!

In July 2007, I again appeared before the VA Oil and Gas Board along with my brother and sister. We had attained a lot of information and had strong and reasonable testimonies (will supply upon request). We gave the board what we felt were powerful legal, civil, and constitutional reasons not to forcibly take our gas from under the land we have legally owned for seventy-seven years. Our plea fell on deaf ears, and the board passed a FORCED POOLING ORDER, which allows Equitable Gas to install equipment on adjacent land to remove the gas from under our land.

At that point my soul and spirit became sick. I took to my bed for four days with physical and emotional pain. I felt I no longer lived in America: "THE LAND OF THE FREE AND THE HOME OF THE BRAVE." I realized the government could, and had, just stripped away my rights and the rights of others. I realized Virginia is no longer a Commonwealth. A government "FOR THE PEOPLE AND BY THE PEOPLE" IS A MYTH. My strong belief that justice will prevail has been shaken to the core. "THESE ARE TIMES THAT TRY MEN'S [AND WOMEN'S] SOULS" (Thomas Paine) seems so profound at this time.

After receiving stringent medical attention, I again picked up my sword. If I don't fight this bully, who will? My spirit is broken but not destroyed. So I move on with my story.

photo by Juanita Sneeuwjagt

A Virginia gas well protrudes from the earth
through a pool of bright orange chemical soup

According to the gas company contracts, the gas companies operating in Southwest Virginia offer the land owner $1.00 (one) to $20.00 (twenty) dollars per acre for a land lease and offer the landowners one eighth of twelve and a half percent for their natural or coal bed methane gas. The gas companies get to keep eighty-seven and one half percent!! A poor attempt is made to locate the heirs or rightful landowners and the percentage promised by the gas companies is put into escrow. At the March 2008 meeting of the VA Oil and Gas Board, the report was that $18,000,000.00 (eighteen million dollars) now sits in the escrow fund.

In October 2007, I organized a meeting to discuss the various abuses spilled onto the landowners by gas companies. Roughly fifty folks attended from Virginia, West Virginia, Ohio, North and South Carolina. Stories shared were from outright theft, contracts broken, land abuse without landowners' consent, illegal rights of way, lack of promised compensation, (usually resulting in pennies or often nothing), destruction of environment, destruction of natural water supplies and the digging of gas wells in family cemeteries. In addition there are injection wells in this county that add toxins to the air and land. All injustices too numerous to mention at this writing.

Several concerned citizens and I have appealed to our legislatures, county and state authorities. We are told since there is a law in place to collect the gas, there is nothing that can be done. Virginia's governor has gone on record stating that every inch of gas under the land must be obtained.

In early Autumn, 2007, the Dickenson County's only newspaper, *The Dickenson Star,* reported that Equitable Gas was in the process of making a deal with the Dickenson County Board of Supervisors and IDA.

The talks seem to have been initiated by the then County Administrator and/or IDA. The County Administrator told me bringing the gas company to this county was his idea. Soon after, three of the County supervisors came on board with deal making plans with Equitable.

Having gotten information about the "deal" contents, I spoke before the Dickenson County Board of Supervisors and the County Administrator pleading with them not to finalize the "deal" because it would jeopardize landowner's rights plus the civil and constitutional rights of most of the county citizens. The environment would certainly never recover.

I then met with the County Administrator and told him I felt he (they) were "making a deal with the devil." I gave him some news, which I'm certain he already possessed. I spoke of the projected number of gas wells, pipelines, and holding tanks that Equitable planned for Dickenson County, which were in excess of five thousand wells alone. I voiced my concerns of the raping and gutting of the land. I spoke of rich gas companies growing richer and the county growing poorer. He responded that most of the mineral rights had been sold long ago. That much is true. During my research, I found that landowners in the early eighteen hundreds to the middle nineteen hundreds had been duped of their mineral rights by coal company owners. Often mineral rights were falsely obtained by giving illiterate landowners as little as twenty-five cents! However, many landowners still own the minerals under their land and at no time has the landowners given up the rights to have a say about the treatment or encroachment of their land.

After going to North Carolina for several weeks, I discovered upon my return that on December 6, 2007, the Dickenson County Board of Supervisors, the County Administrator, and the IDA had closeted themselves with Equitable Gas Production and had made a honey of a "deal" with Equitable Gas being the primary beneficiary. The deal terms are as follows: Equitable Gas was given nineteen acres in Dickenson County to the tune of $450,000.00. Furthermore, a contract was signed by the aforementioned parties to give to Equitable Gas one hundred thousand dollars each year for five years. These generous presents are in exchange for three-percent tax revenue to be showered on Dickenson County. Dickenson County does not have that kind of money in the coffers, so in all likelihood that financial burden will lie on the county taxpayers.

In December 2007, I attended the last Board of Supervisors meeting of the year, indeed, the last meeting of the members of that board. I spoke before the board and asked what the Dickenson County citizens might receive in return for the magnanimous bequests to Equitable Gas. The Board Chairman put up his hand in the universal sign for "halt" and said the Board had made no deal or contract, that I should take my concerns to the IDA. Of course IDA was just one player in the triumverate. At the meeting conclusion, the Board Chairperson was encapsulating the Board accomplishments and ended his pontification stating that the Board had made a deal with Equitable Gas to locate their Regional Headquarters in Dickenson County. He stated that the county would probably not realize a profit from Equitable for the first five years, at which time Equitable's contract will expire leaving the County "holding the bag." The recent Board of Supervisors has sold the County down the river.

On January 15, 2008, I attended the Virginia Oil and Gas Board meeting after several months of absence. Mostly it was the same old song and dance. What I had not realized before was that at the end of the monthly meeting there is a segment for public comment.

At the January 15, 2008, meeting, a renowned geologist by the name of Dr. Charles Bartlett testified that he had been the caretaker of an estate in Dickenson County since 1990. On that estate were gas wells, etc. Dr. Bartlett has kept scrupulous records pertaining to royalties and taxes. According to his documentation Dr. Bartlett found numerous discrepancies in the amount of royalties paid to his clients by Equitable Gas and the amount reported to the state of Virginia. The Virginia Oil and Gas Board requested an investigation by Equitable Gas. Equitable's Vice President and Chief Counselor, Kevin West, stated that no error has been made by Equitable. Dr. Bartlett asked Mr. West since his clients were paid more than was reported to VA State that perhaps his clients should return some of the money. Mr. West responded that the clients could keep the money. Dr. Bartlett posed questions relating to what point did Equitable pay royalties to mineral owners: Was it at well head production? Was it after transportation costs? Was it after using some of the gas for compressors? Mr. West chose to remain silent and not answer Dr. Bartlett's questions.

During a winter day in January 2008, three plumbers were doing exterior work for me and came to tell me that they smelled very strong gas odors on the east side of my house. I called Equitable's land man, Don Hall, on his cell phone. He did not have an emergency number I could call! He said to call the office in the morning! It took me seven calls to find an emergency number to report this. This county has such an intricate gas line network that if there should be a gas line fire this county would blow to extinction.

The various gas companies in Southwest Virginia are out of control, and no one I have spoken with is willing to put out a foot to trip them up. They seem accountable to no one. I smell corruption from the top to the bottom and all stops in between. There appears to be a network of "good ole" boys in control of the money, the power and the jobs. I'm told they do not hesitate to dish out retribution to anyone hindering their path.

Mostly I am fearful of losing the remainder of our civil and constitutional rights. I am very frightened of losing the natural environments the clean water supplies, and the ecosystems. I am frightened of losing the simple pleasures I hold dear so rich companies can grow richer, and thrown into the mix, no one seems to know if the natural and coal bed methane gas procured by the gas companies will even stay in the United States to sustain us. Adding insult to injury, there appears to be no land reclamation law that applies to gas companies. Come take a look at the devastation! You will weep!

Lacking is any sense of moral standards by the state or federal government. The foundation of our leadership now appears to be based on self-accumulation of wealth and/or power. We can no longer appeal to our legislators for help. Their actions serve to assist big business in achieving their goals. The average person has been stripped of civil and constitutional rights. As A taxpaying, law abiding, upstanding citizen, I have a right to have rights!!

I beseech you! Pick up the banner and march with me! Let's take back the right to live in the dignity of quiet possession.

photo by Delilah O'Haynes

Coal Tipple

One Artist's View

by Wilma Lee Steele

Nature has always been important to me. When I was a child, camping and fishing with my family were a major part of summertime. My own special place was a vine-covered tree canopy where it was always cool and many good books were my only companions.

As an adult, my husband and I share the love of time spent together in the hills. We love West Virginia and our hearts grieve over what is happening here. I am often asked, "Ms. Steele, have you seen the golf course or the trails? Don't you like them? I have seen them, the hatchery, the industrial park, the plans for the school and much more. I am not against progress and if the mountaintop has already been blasted apart, then good use for what is left is great.

Now, I ask you, "Have you seen what was there before? Do you know what we just destroyed?" These mountains are one of the oldest mountain ranges in the world. Many of our families have been in this country since before the Revolutionary war or even earlier. Our connection with the Appalachians is a part of our heritage. Every cliff had a name, and animals and plants were our means of survival. I know times have changed, but to destroy so much of our heritage for money is a shame. So I ask you, "Have you looked down on these mountains from a plane and seen just how much is gone? Have you seen the flooding and destruction of your neighbor's property with the third 100-year rain?"

I've heard an "act of God" once too often! I do what others have done in the past when their eyes and ears have witnessed loss of too much—I use my art to create, I write words to cry out, and I pray that someone hears. I support those that do something to stop the wrong that is being done.

Art is not just pretty pictures—many of its images are quite disturbing, but it has the ability to get others to be still and see. Our writers, singers, moviemakers, painters and sculptors have always been important to social change. Their works are often the consciousness-expanding voice that gets others to hear.

I do not put myself in this great company or on that level. I am only another heart that cares. I know I have friends that have a stronger talent and ability than mine, but when small groups of passionate people join together for a common good—then mountains move—or stay.

photo by Delilah O'Haynes

Appalachian Waterfall

A Day in the Life of Walk for the Mountains
Thursday August 12, 1999

by Vivian Stockman

Revving up Kayford Mountain in my friend's little convertible after two in the morning verged on madness, but how else were we supposed to squeeze in time to watch the Perseid meteor showers? Bats swooped above us, lucky to have food and habitat here in West Virginia's southern coalfields.

Around Kayford, mountaintop removal operations have turned square mile after square mile of forests, streams, mountains and valleys into dusty piles of lifeless rock; forlorn man-made deserts created for short-term profit without regard for the future. Here and there patches of "reclaimed" land sport grasses that not even cattle will eat. Scrubs trees grow on a very few spots. But the vibrant diversity of life that once graced the coalfields' decapitated mountains will not return, at least not for centuries.

Before we ascended the mountain, coal trucks were passing us every few minutes. On the steep road up, we pulled aside to allow two coal trucks to pass. Their brakes screamed eerily under the load, and dust boiled all around us, a whiteout at night. Do the trucks never cease carting away the heart of the mountains?

At the summit of Kayford, we saw only one other vehicle besides Larry Gibson's. It looked like, come daylight, the "Walk for the Mountains" wouldn't have many walkers as we traversed Cabin Creek, the hollow where so many people depend on coal mining for their livelihood.

We stretched our camping mats under a shelter, so that we could watch the sky for meteors. Soon, I could hear DL Hamilton's steady sleep-breathing. Hoping to fall asleep, too, I tried to concentrate on the gentle nighttime woods-song of katydids and crickets. But a continuous low, loud rumble interspersed with the groaning and beep beep beep of backing vehicles kept me awake. The screech of brakes on coal trucks echoed up the mountain like some sort of tortured whale song. Every half hour or so, pick up trucks, many in need of new mufflers, roared passed our sleeping shelter. I learned later that workers at the mountaintop removal sites around Kayford must travel up and over the mountain to get to work at all hours of the day and night. At first light I gave up the struggle to sleep, getting up to wait for Larry.

In the morning, Larry emerged from his cousin's modest shelter, glad to see more people ready to join the walk. His overnight guest was Rick Eades, a hydrogeologist with WV Citizens Action Group. Larry and Rick had talked late into the night about the walk, worried because a handful of miners had promised to rough-up Larry if he walked through Cabin Creek.

Some coal miners blame "environmentalists" for layoffs. Legal challenges to mountaintop removal operations have resulted in the suspension of work at some mountaintop removal mines. For decades, governmental regulators and mine operators have failed to follow state and federal mining laws. For the past 20 years, the coal industry has been replacing workers with big machines to increase profits. The economies of some southern counties depend almost entirely on coal, with little economic diversification. Despite coal company claims of providing prosperity, these same counties have the highest poverty rates and some of the worst infrastructure and school systems in the state.

Both men went to sleep recalling the miner's threats of violence and wondering if others would join the walk on Thursday. As day dawned, Rick recalled the Native American philosophy summed up by the phrase, "Today is a good day to die." As we pondered that, another vehicle arrived on Kayford's summit. Novelist, outspoken mountaintop removal opponent and gubernatorial candidate Denise Giardina and her campaign manager Vince George would join us on the walk.

Caffeinated, we drove down the mountain to the Kayford Freewill Baptist Church, about the only structure left in the "town". We waited for others who had promised to walk. Long minutes passed. As coal trucks rumbled by, each of us swallowed hard, thinking about passing the Samples Mine entrance. That's where the miners who had promised to beat up Larry worked. We didn't worry long, though, as walkers began appearing to join us. Soon twenty people gathered at the church, including James and Sibby Weekly, Blair residents who are litigants on the lawsuit. Like Larry, they have been harassed and intimidated for daring to take a stand against the eco-slaughter. Channel 8 news showed up, and later a Channel 13 news crew joined us.

We gathered up the state flag and a "Stop Mountaintop Removal" sign. We trod the first steps of a six-hour-long walk from Kayford to Sharon, along the Cabin Creek hollow, overshadowed by a line of steep mountains, some not as steep as they used to be. Their height blocked us from seeing the mining operations that were scouring the landscape all around us. We estimated that at least 150 coal trucks passed us as we walked on the edge of the narrow road. The trucks, weighing about 30 tons empty and up to 100 tons full, lumbered over little bridges where signs indicate a weight limit of 8 or 12 tons. Many coal trucks far exceed the legal weight limits. At least 50 other trucks rolled by, each one pummeling the asphalt as they carried fuel, explosives and pieces of huge equipment to the mine sites.

photo by Kent Kessinger

Appalachian Vista

Our steps were buoyed by the presence of four young teenagers and three even younger kids. Most of the kids used to live in Kayford and Red Warrior communities that, as the mining intensified, shriveled like the mountains around them. Larry told the kids he was walking for them, for their futures.

We waved to the coal truck drivers. One coal truck driver purposely buzzed us, but all the rest swung wide. We were well aware that we were making their job more difficult, so we walked as far from the road as we could. Some drivers gave us the finger. Most ignored us, but a surprising number waved back. Perhaps they shared the sentiment of a worker at a coal tipple, where a coal train slowly lumbered, creaking and groaning and spewing dust as coal crashed into the empty cars. "I don't like mountaintop removal either," he shouted at us across the street, "but it's my job!"

None of us disagreed that jobs were at stake. But all of the walkers knew that, at most, there's only about 30 years worth of jobs left for an ever-decreasing number of workers. (Studies say that at the current rate of extraction, West Virginia's coal reserves will be gone in about 27 years.) The destruction wrought now will last centuries, at the very least. The entire family of one teenager who walked with us said her five members of her family are employed at the Samples mine. Still, she walked because she knows there is no future in mountaintop removal. She walked because she has seen what mountaintop removal has done to her hometown.

In one community, a pastor painting his church steeple called to offer us a drink of water. He had been up all night working in a deep mine, and had come directly from work to paint his church. Like people all along the route, he offered us words of encouragement. In Cabin Creek, where many depend on mountaintop removal for jobs, the sentiment against it runs strong. If you live in the shadow of this kind of mining, you know what it means.

After ten miles of walking, we stopped for the day. We were all so hot and our leg muscles twitched, but the discomfort didn't matter. We were elated at the support we had received, right here in the heart of coal country.

Denise, Vince, Rick—all West Virginia natives—and I (hey, my granny and grandpa were from West Virginia) went back up to Kayford to look at the mine sites. Clouds of dust from blasting muddied the sky. We looked out over miles of destruction, unable to distinguish what had been valleys from what had been mountains. After long minutes of sullen silence, Denise began to sing "Oh, the West Virginia Hills…" Vince and Rick joined her and the song grew louder. The song had no mountains and valleys through which to echo. But about a week later, 200 people celebrated the last day of the Walk for the Mountains by singing that song on the State Capitol grounds. It will echo in the heart of all those people as they do their part to stop mountaintop removal.

photo by Paul Corbit Brown

Mountaintop Removal Mining

Mountaintop Removal

by Vivian Stockman

This hollow is like so many others—a twisted, narrow ribbon of fertile bottomland separating the steep, convoluted mountains of Southern West Virginia. Here, as in all these valleys, it's easy to see that this sheltering, isolating landscape molded the culture of the Appalachian folk as they made a living off what they could harvest both from above and below the ground.

A rock-strewn stream meanders through the hollow. Minnows dart in and out of the shade cast by elderberry bushes, scrubby willows and a trio of sycamores, their upper trunks nearly all white. Come autumn, a woman will pick the elderberries for a cobbler made from a recipe given to her mother by her grandmother. Each of them grew up in this hollow, sharing with the birds the berries from these same bushes.

A pickerel frog, perhaps startled by a muskrat, springs in a graceful arc from the bank into the cold water with barely a splash. The flute-like trill of a wood thrush floats out from the branches of a stream-bank dogwood that, in response to its prime edge habitat, spreads wider and taller than its counterparts in the woods.

A tidy farmhouse sits alongside a little brook that flows into the bigger stream. Here, it's just a few yards before the gardens and clipped lawn surrounding the house give way to the dense thickets of hazelnut, blackberry and blooming multiflora rose, marking the dark edge of the woods. A deer bounds into this maze, and disappears within seconds. Now, in late May, the landscape is utterly dominated by a breeze-tossed wall of many shades of green—the leaves of scores of different kinds of trees, each rooted in the unfathomably ancient soil of the Appalachian Mountains. The tree-covered slopes rise hundreds of feet above the hollow, so that only a sliver of perfect azure sky, complete with cotton candy clouds, is visible from the old homeplace.

Inside the woods, life expresses itself in myriad ways—this is the mixed mesophytic forest, home to one of the most richly diverse plant communities of all temperate climates on earth. A recent shower has tumbled the last tulip tree flowers to the forest floor. Earthy soil scents mingle with the light, fruity aroma of the blossoms. The heart-shaped leaves of the wood violet tell of wildflowers missed, while a late bluet sways in the slightest breeze. Sunlight dapples the yellow-green fronds of maidenhair ferns, as they bob on delicate black stalks below a towering white oak. Velvety, emerald green moss and scaly gray-green lichen carpet a sandstone boulder that serves as a resting perch for anyone making her way through the forest.

The diversity of the woods shapes the activities of local people's lives. In early spring, folks gather ramps and greens for tonics—an internal spring-cleaning. Molly moochers, or morels, reward the sharp-eyed person who knows the exact moment in spring when rainfall will sprout these delicacies from the damp soil. The seasons, too, dictate when one should scramble about the steep woods, hunting herbs like black cohosh and ginseng, both for personal medicines and for some cash income. Locals pluck wintergreen from its creepings along the forest floor and dig the roots of sassafras saplings to flavor mugs of aromatic tea. They harvest fallen trees and fell hardwoods for firewood and lumber. In fall, black walnut and hickories feed animals of the two- and four-legged variety. Some of those four-leggeds fall to the hunter's gun, providing protein for families throughout the winter. After the first freeze, people shake the persimmon tree for its custard-like fruits that dangle with an offer of sweet sustenance. So the woods cycle through the seasons, from stark winter to lush summer jungle.

Back down in the hollow, people resting on the front porch mark the onset of a spring evening by the increased nattering of a catbird mimicking its cousins. As twilight fades into night, the whippoorwill, named for its song, begins its repetitive call.

This was the beauty, serenity and bounty of this hollow up until a few years ago. Now, the whippoorwill's cry no longer heralds dusk and few people remain to live within this landscape's seasonal rhythms. Some days, the last few folks can still hear the melodious songs of the ever-dwindling number of birds, the bubbling of the brooks and the whisperings of the leaves. Other days, when the wind blows differently, the blasts and mechanical rumblings and beeps of nearby destruction shatter the soundscape. The din draws ever closer—a noisy foreboding of the annihilation heading this way.

Profit-crazed coal companies that practice mountaintop removal / valley fill coal mining are coming to claim this hollow, despite the objections of the people who want to stay on the land they love…people who, so far, have resisted the buyout offers. Long ago, their ancestors, deceived by the slick talk and of company reps, signed away their rights to the coal deposits beneath their land. Of course, those ancestors could never have conceived of mountaintop removal.

For over a century, the coal has been mined from the ground beneath these hills and hollows. For many families living here, the mining jobs provided cash that helped buy what the land could not offer. That cash came with a toll, as tens of thousands of miners died from accidents, or from black lung disease, or from battling the companies in order to establish unions. The coal industry promised prosperity, but the wealth was mostly whisked out of state. To this day, the majority of West Virginians have very little monetary wealth compared to folks in other states.

Sadly, now the area's most important natural wealth—the forests, the streams and the culture—is being devastated so that companies can get more coal, more quickly and more cheaply, with far fewer miners. The moonscapes—the biological deserts—that are the aftermath of mountaintop removal have come to Southern West Virginia, Eastern Kentucky, and, to a limited degree, portions of Virginia and Tennessee.

To get to the multiple, thin layers of low-sulfur coal that underlie these mountains, coal companies first raze the verdant forests, scraping away the topsoil and its priceless bank of seeds. In a mad dash to get to the coal, the trees are usually shoved out of the way, not even harvested as lumber. The understory herbs like ginseng and goldenseal are trashed with an arrogant disregard for their current worth, let alone their value to future generations.

Up to 800 feet of denuded mountaintops and the underlying rock is then systematically blown up. The explosives used can register anywhere from 10 to 100 times the strength of the explosion that tore open the Oklahoma City Federal Building. The blasts send health-endangering, silica-laden dust into the air. The shock waves can travel miles from the site, sometimes ferociously rattling the foundations of homes, as well as people's nerves. The blasting has affected groundwater, drying up wells or ruining the taste and color of the water. "Fly rock," more aptly named *fly boulder*, can occasionally rain off the blasting sites, endangering residents' homes and lives.

The layers of coal are then scooped out by giant draglines, up to 20 stories tall. Behemoth dump trucks cart hundreds of millions of tons of "overburden"—the former mountaintops—to the narrow, adjacent valleys. The trucks dump the rubble over the sides, filling the valleys and burying the headwaters streams, which scientists say provide habitat for an unusually high diversity of aquatic organisms. These critters act as the biological engines that drive the life downstream. Across Appalachia, according to a draft environmental impact statement on mountaintop removal, valley fills already have buried forever 724 miles of streams and have negatively impacted a total of 1,200 stream miles. Some aquatic biologists argue that the figure is much greater, and that the destruction more harmful than most people realize. Selenium is just one toxic metal that has been found in high concentrations in the water seeping from valley fills.

Already, mountaintop removal has claimed nearly 400,000 acres of forested mountains. Entire communities, built long ago in hollows the companies now desire for valley fills, have been bought out. For other communities, mountaintop removal grinds ever closer, and worries about the blasting damages become almost routine, as even bigger problems claim attention. Every time it rains, folks who live close to this greed-crazed form of mining get scared. Really scared.

Government studies have shown that valley fills can dramatically worsen floods associated with heavy summer thunderstorms. Residents really didn't need these studies to back up their experience—thousands of acres of bulldozed-away forests, blown-up mountains and rubble-filled valleys just don't handle rain like intact ecosystems do. In Southern West Virginia, flooding in 2001 and 2002 killed 15 people, destroyed thousands of homes and damaged thousands more. Recovery efforts so far have topped $150 million. Residents blame mountaintop removal and virtually unregulated logging for making the floods far worse than they would have been without these disturbances.

Floods don't just come off valleys fills. Mountaintop removal generates huge amounts of waste. While the solid waste becomes the fills, the liquid waste, created when coal is washed and processed for market, is stored in massive slurry impoundments that loom above communities. These lakes of slurry contain water contaminated with a black, toxic brew of carcinogenic chemicals—used to wash the coal—as well as particles laden with all the heavy metals found in coal, including arsenic and mercury. Several times a year, water plant operators are forced to shut down drinking water intake valves as upstream waters are blackened by spills from coal processing plants and sludge impoundments.

In 2000, the floor of one coal sludge impoundment near Inez, Ky., partially broke through into an abandoned underground mine. Over 300 million gallons of sludge spewed into people's yards, in some places up to fifteen feet deep, and fouled 75 miles of waterways. Several similar impoundments still sit above schools and towns. People believe it's a matter of "when" not "if" for the next disaster. They fearfully wonder if, this time, someone will be killed.

For years, while coal companies have had their way with the coalfields, both state and federal regulators have failed to enforce mining laws that would rein in some of the worst abuses. Many politicians, secure in the coal industry's pocket, have ignored requests for help. Feeling under siege, people mourn the loss of their homeplaces. They question the wisdom of those who can rationalize such devastation as necessary for meeting the nation's "cheap" energy needs. And, they turn to each other for answers.

With the help of West Virginia environmental groups like the Ohio Valley Environmental Coalition, Coal River Mountain Watch, and West Virginia Highlands Conservancy, people are rising up to demand an end to this ecocidal form of coal mining. They organize, educate, litigate—thanks to the Appalachian Center for the Environment, Earthjustice and Public Justice—and strategize to save what is left of the central Appalachian forest.

We are making strides to save this land and our people. Please join us.

photo by Vivian Stockman

Erosion of "Reclaimed" MTR Site

photo by Vivian Stockman

Erosion of MTR Site

Statement of James Tawney
Nicholas County, West Virginia, March, 2008

by James Tawney

recorded and transcribed by Delilah F. O'Haynes

James Tawey works to make Broad Rights Deeds illegal. They are illegal in Ky now. Severance deeds can have what they call "reservations," which give logging and mining companies broad rights. People buying land in Appalachia that isn't in Ky should check the deed for such reservations.

The following reservation was attached to James Tawney's land back in 1904 but did not show up on the regular deed: *"exclusive right to enter upon said land and make all necessary roads, ways, pipelines, excavations, shafts and air shafts, drain ways, wells, structures and opening necessary or desirable for the mining or removal of said coal and other minerals and mineral substances, including oil and gas, from said land and from adjoining and other lands to market, without being liable for any injury done."*

We, me and my wife, worked our butts off for this property. I had a lawn care service, and she was a secretary. We worked and saved until we finally saved up enough to buy our property. We have about a 120-acre farm.

I was outside one evening, and I kept hearing dozers. I kept thinking, well, they're not gonna come over on my side, so I didn't really think much about it. This went on for like a month, and probably two weeks after it stopped, I went up on the ridge to check out what was going on and I seen a road cut through my property. It just floored me; I couldn't believe it. I've got posted signs up there every twenty or thirty foot.

So I called the forester, and I said, "Someone's up here logging on my property without permission." And he said, "No, there ain't nobody up there logging. Let me call around and make sure." He called me back and said, "I couldn't find no one. You ain't mistaking that logging road for a core drilling site, are you?"

I called the land office and asked, and they said they'd cut a core-drilling road up there. I said, "Well, you cut across my property." He said, "We're sorry about that. The guy got out there and didn't have his maps with him and got lost." I said, "Well, you tore some trees up and built a road. You'll have to pay for the damage and reclaim it." He said, "We'll pay for everything. We want to be good neighbors to you."

He met me up on top of the ridge and said, "You go get a forester and tell him what trees you lost and everything. We want to take care of you." He shook my hand. I took that as good. They did get a violation by the DEP for being off their bonded area and being on there without a permit because it was a prospecting permit—they wasn't supposed to go up that way.

We kept waiting and no response. So I kind of got upset. I was like, well, you know they need to make a decision. They'd used my land for this long and tore the timber up and needed to pay for it. They sent us a letter from a lawyer in Tennessee. He stated there was a "reservation" in the original deed—from 1904—saying we had 93 acres of land & mineral rights and 27.4 acres where we owned the land but not the mineral rights. He said they could use our land without notice and could tear down as many trees as they wanted to, take as much rock as they wanted to, as much water as they wanted to, wherever they wanted to do the mining process without compensation at all.

After that I tried to get a hold of lawyers. It's kind of hard to get a lawyer to fight for you for $1500 worth of trees. It's hard to find someone to take up for you unless you've got the money. That's why I'm trying to get broad rights' deeds illegal in West Virginia. It's illegal in Kentucky. There they at least have to have the permission of the land owner. If you pay taxes on surface land, you should have as much say about what happens to that land as the person that owns the mineral rights.

We've been doing this for two years, and it's almost took over my life. It's got to the point to where—I took land that I loved and I fought for—it's made me feel like I've got to watch my land all the time. If I don't, someone's gonna come in here and do whatever they want to, and I can't fight it.

The water issue is the thing I worry about because if they can come up there and do whatever they want to my creek—my creek is like my life blood. If you ain't got control of your water, you don't got control of nothing underneath, even though it's the surface owner who pays the taxes. I've got a well, but I actually drink out of a spring. It's the best water. If they come up there, I know they'll ruin it.

photo by Kent Kessinger

Mountain Stream

I've got a beautiful view of the Gauley River. I wanted to develop my land. I thought I could build an observation tower on the ridge, and a campground for all the rafters, and build a ski lodge and rent it out—and there's my income. There's thousands of people comes in there in the summertime. But why would I spend my money and my time trying to develop my land? Who's gonna come up there to view the river and then turn to the right and see a big old high wall on the other side?

Everything I say is my opinion about them. I don't care a bit to say they're crooked, crooked and corrupt. Anyone who'll say they're gonna be a good neighbor and then a month or two later pull up a broad rights deed with a "reservation" clause and hand it to you. I've GOT to be on the lookout for 'em all the time. I gotta be in there looking for the permit or they'll renew it. They can just renew a permit and you can't hardly stop a renewal.

I'm dreading the day when I do see a permit because I've challenged 'em on the selenium and the Gauley River. There ain't much hope of stopping it, but at least they'll see that there's high selenium going into the river. Maybe that'll give me a bit more standing. In high doses, selenium kills aquatic life and can harm humans. It's sad to see what they're doing in our area. I mean, I know a lot of other areas have a LOT of mining, like Boone and Logan. But I think Nicholas and Clay are the forgotten areas.

I never considered myself an environmentalist. I've cut trees all my life—logging. But environmentalists are the only people you can go to who'll help you. Everything—logging, coal—can be done right. Before mountaintop removal, they left the mountains. It's greed. They take off a whole mountain for six to eight inches of coal. I'm thinking, the timber on that mountain, even if you just used a piece at a time—select timbering—will be worth probably three or four times in its life more than that coal ever would be. But they want to make quick money and get it while they can, while they've got the permits. Be damned to everybody else—who cares? That's how they look at it. The law is scared of 'em. Money. Money and politics. I hear a lot of people say the workers have to have their money. I don't care. I mean, my dad was a miner. You do stuff to make money, but you don't do things that hurts others to make money.

So is it gonna be a physical battle up there instead of a legal battle? Is it going to come to that—to where I gotta protect my timberland? There comes a point where someone's gonna have to stand up and say, "No more, you ain't gonna take it," and set a precedence for everybody else. There isn't too many people who actually speak up. I call it gutless. If somebody's got the guts to stand up there and say, "Either you're gonna kill me or you're not gonna do it," maybe they'd stop. But I don't see it. They'd look at that person as a terrorist—stopping "Progress." They'd say, "Let's put him in jail."

I'll protect my land like a game protector. How else am I gonna fight it, unless I go over there and tell 'em, "Hey, you can't come up here—I ain't letting you. Either you're gonna take me off this tree I'm chained to or kill me." It's sad that it would come down to the point where I even gotta think that way. I bought that land to live there and die. That's my dream. I'm tired of giving up.

photo by Delilah O'Haynes

Virginia Vista

Mountaintop Removal

by Seth Taylor

For far too long, mountaintop removal, also known as surface mining and strip mining, has ravaged our nation's beautiful countryside in a foolish search for coal. Strip mining leaves delicate ecosystems desolate and annihilates any and all usefulness of the land in the future. This practice has decimated and disintegrated more resources than it has foolishly obtained and must be stopped immediately and permanently through smart energy usage, environmental preservation, and pollution elimination.

Strip mining is defined as: "Removing a mineral deposit from the Earth after first removing the layer of earth above it. Strip mining, the cheapest method of mining, is also the most controversial, because it jeopardizes the environment, and because strip-mined land is either expensive or impossible to reclaim" ("Strip Mining"). Like a putrid, festering scar on the face of the land, strip mining wreaks havoc upon the pristine beauty of the mountainous terrain and the people of the now desolate land's shattered remains are left to deal with the devastation. "An overwhelming majority of those aware of the environmental destruction wrought by mountaintop removal coal mining are opposed to the practice" (Scheer). The strip mines tear through the land like tornadoes, only they are much, much worse because not only are these travesties unnecessary and preventable, but the lands affected are also virtually irreparable. "There are stiff ecological and environmental prices to pay for reaping the earth's geologic riches so easily. Surface mining in the western states occurs over thousands of acres. In Wyoming, companies hold permits to mine more than 320,000 acres, although not all of that area is likely to be mined. A few hundred acres may be dug up, and, when that is played out, the company moves on to another patch of land covered by the permit" (Gillis). These digs leave more and more craterous pockmarks that disfigure our dear environment.

The destruction wrought by stripping the land disturbs various precious ecosystems. "With an economy which has been tied to natural resource extraction, primarily coal, gas, and timber, the Appalachian region of eastern Kentucky has experienced significant disturbance of its environment" (Nieman and Merkin). Human suffering is also a result of the plague of mountaintop removal. "Communities have borne real costs in lost land productivity, property damage, degraded water quality, and health and safety impacts" (Nieman and Merkin). Until the 1977 Surface Mining Control and Reclamation Act, "the preservation or protection of flora and fauna had been virtually ignored in the pursuit of coal resources" but the damage so unthinkingly incurred upon the land was already done (Nieman and Merkin). Regulations have been set in attempts to lessen the effects of surface mining on the delicate environment. "Regulations require that mining companies gather an enormous quantity of environmental data for the mining-permit application. Monitoring of environmental conditions, particularly ground and surface water quality, is also required during the mining process and through the bond period" (Nieman and Merkin). Although these implementations have been placed to try to lessen the damages on the surroundings, the damage created is still very evident. "Regulations are a response to past negligence and abuse of the environment" (Nieman and Merkin). Yet, with these new regulations, the negligence still persists. The regulations in place are much too lenient and companies get away with flouting the set parameters and yet the surface mining companies consider the regulations "too rigid" (Nieman and Merkin).

Coal is one of the most commonly strip-mined minerals. "Coal was discovered in the eastern United States soon after colonization, and large scale extraction commenced shortly thereafter" (Baller and Pantilat). Coal is a great asset to the United States of America, providing jobs as well as the energy for electricity across the entire nation; however, with the current tools being utilized in burning coal, the benefits of coal are far outweighed by the greenhouse gases that it creates. "Burning coal is a leading source of global warming pollution" ("The Facts"). The pollution caused by coal, coupled with the environmental decimation of strip mining is a combination that will surely cause various ecological and environmental problems for many future generations. "Mountaintop removal also harms the surrounding communities that have lived in the mountains for generations. Residents near mines suffer from 'rock slides, catastrophic floods, poisoned water supplies, constant blasting, destroyed property, and lost culture'" (Baller and Pantilat). These problems can be averted, if not completely removed, by the implementation of "green" technologies, technologies that produce energy at little to no expense to the environment. These technologies are available but are not being implemented simply because the population is not willing to make the lifestyle changes needed to make the world a better place for upcoming generations. "We have the technical know-how to use less energy per capita and retain a reasonable standard of living, but we do not appear to have the will to implement such a plan" (Letcher). In order to keep up with America's energy wants, mining businesses implement the cheapest method of mining to keep up with the demand; they foolishly do this to make quick, easy money, not focusing on long term affects that will surely hail down upon the already stressed environment. "Burning coal is the dirtiest way we produce energy [...] there are roughly 600 coal plants producing electricity in the U.S. Not one of them captures and stores its global warming pollution" ("The Facts"). If rewards were given to the people and corporations that used less environmentally harmful energy and corporations that pollute were fined much more harshly for their outright foolishness, focus could then be shifted toward technology that is ecologically friendly so that strip mining could be completely eliminated, thus eradicating the burden it so generously bestows upon the environment. The jobs created by the clean energy industries would also eliminate any jobs lost by the abolition of surface mining.

The solution to the ecological problems directly caused by strip mining is to completely and utterly abolish the practice of mountaintop removal and replace the practice with technologies that, when applied, are environmentally friendly and effective. The scarring that strip mining has already made may be irreversible; therefore the practice should be stopped. The ruination of the environment is no price that the population should have to pay for energy that may be obtained elsewhere. The abolishing of strip mining is imperative for our environment to be healthy, unspoiled, and pristine and, with several simple applications; the horrid practice of mountaintop removal can be rendered obsolete.

Works cited —

Baller, Mark, and Leor Joseph Pantilat. "Defenders of Appalachia: the campaign to eliminate mountaintop removal coal mining and the role of Public Justice." *Environmental Law* 37.3 (Summer 2007): 629(35). Academic OneFile. Infotrac. Concord University Marsh Library. 12 December 2008.
Gillis, Anna Maria. "Bringing back the land." *BioScience* 41.n2 (Feb 1991): 68(4). Academic OneFile. Infotrac. Concord University Marsh Library. 12 December 2008.
Letcher, Trevor. "Future energy: improved, sustainable, and clean options for our planet. (The Project Place)." *Chemistry International* 30.2 (March-April 2008): 20(2). Academic OneFile. Infotrac. Concord University Marsh Library. 12 December 2008.
Nieman, Thomas J., and Zina R. Merkin. "Wildlife management, surface mining, and regional planning." *Growth and Change* 26.n3 (Summer 1995): 405(20). Academic OneFile. Infotrac. Concord University Marsh Library. 12 December 2008.
Scheer, Roddy. "Most oppose mountaintop removal." *Our Planet* (Oct 27, 2008): NA. Academic OneFile. Infotrac. Concord University Marsh Library. 12 December 2008.
"Strip Mining. (Definition)." *The New Dictionary of Cultural Literacy*, 3rd ed.. Houghton Mifflin Harcourt Publishing Company, 2002. NA. Academic OneFile. Infotrac. Concord University Marsh Library. 12 December 2008.
"The Facts." *This is Reality*. 12 December 2008. <http://thisisreality.org>.

Testimony—
Charleston, West Virginia, March, 2008

Cary Huffman, Karen Huffman, Patricia Feeney, James Tawney, Beverly Walkup

recorded and transcribed by Delilah F. O'Haynes

James Tawney explained to the group the difficult situation he has faced with mining groups core drilling on his property; he has no legal recourse since a "reservation" was placed on the deed in the early Twentieth Century allowing such activity by the mining company. (See his statement in this book for more information.)

James: In my mind, the surface owner has controlling rights. You've got your timber rights and your land rights. They've just got the mineral rights. You have more of a controlling interest in the land legally, I would think, than they would. But they look at it differently.

Cary: That's the way it should be. If they take a six-foot seam of coal, then they should put everything back EXACTLY the way it is.

James: Last thing I heard, they're doing six, eight inches. That's what they're doing.

Beverly: In other places, it had to be at least eighteen inches before they would take it. They act like it's national security that they get these little four or five inches of coal out of there, when there are coal reserves that they could tackle and not bother all these people.

Cary: What they're doing with that four or five inches is that they just need it for filler. They mix with this stuff that's not any good to get the high money. We're from Amstead. What we've got is some land, and we're into the tourism industry. We think the mountains—the beauty of the mountains and the hiking and whatever the mountains have to offer tourists—if they take the tops off the mountains, it'll put us out of business. They'll be no body to come to look at the beauty of the mountains and the streams. So we have a list of names—petitions—from people as far away as Deleware. They said, hey, we came here to see the mountains not knowing what was happening. They said, you give us some petitions, and they sent us back two sheets of petitions from people who said, we don't want the mountains taken away in case we want to go down there to look, okay? It makes no sense to me for the state to provide millions of dollars to build Fayette County up to build tourism in this area and then blast the tops of the mountains off so there's nothing for them here to see. What's it going to do ten or fifteen years down the road? When the mountains are gone, so is your tourism. I don't think they're going to come just to ride a river.

Beverly: I'm also involved in tourism. I own a little art gallery that's my income from now on. I don't want to give these guys a job for just a few months if it's going to deprive me or my kids of being able to work there.

Cary: Also, they want to tie it to the income. They say coal mining makes jobs, but I don't really believe that's true because I spent twenty-five years in the mines. I was an underground miner. It seems to me like when I first got into it in the late sixties, early seventies, we had a hundred and twenty-five, hundred and thirty-thousand people in the mines. They were building and had money coming in. But now you have, what, fifteen thousand miners and they're taking more coal. So the only thing they're making jobs for is machinery. Machinery don't pay me anything unless I own it, so I can't buy the argument that the coal companies create jobs. They don't create jobs for the towns that they destroy, and if you're lucky enough to get a job in a town that's been destroyed, you're one of the unlikely few because they bring the operators with them. Once you're on, you'll make a good living with the company. But you don't tear up your livelihood now and expect your kids and grandkids to be able to stay there.

Beverly: If the industry is so great, why is this the poorest state in the nation? They make the rich richer and the poor poorer. And it's leaving nothing as a legacy for our children. We have nothing to leave to them if they're going to tear up the mountains, take the trees, take the minerals, destroy the water, destroy the air. That mountain's full of selenium and silica. It's already killed thousands of men years ago when they dug that tunnel through that mountain. Most of them were men who came from down south that were black. It was the black population that suffered the most. Some of the people don't even know where their men are buried. And what happens on our mountain does not stay there because what's on top of our mountain feeds into the Gauley and the New River, which feeds into the Kanawa and goes onto the Ohio and the Mississippi and the Gulf Stream. And that mercury is ending up in our seafood.

Cary: See, if we have enough silica in a mountain to kill thousands of people, then what happens when someone blows the top off the mountains? There's no way to capture that, that I can see, so not only are we going to breathe it, but it's also going to filter down and go into these streams. You know what coal-miners' black lung is? It comes off the sandstone. It's the same thing. Silica tears your lungs up.

Beverly: It makes your lungs hard like cement. And the selenium: The CDC put out a warning against people taking so many selenium supplements because it might cause diabetes. We have a high percentage of people with diabetes, and selenium is in the water supply. They've already issued a warning that you can't eat the fish because of the selenium rate, and it makes you wonder about the water going into the homes. They're not even checking for selenium, and there's a high rate of diabetes in West Virginia.

Karen: There's diabetes, high blood pressure, and other diseases.

Cary: And a high incidence of cancer.

Beverly: And MS. I'm suffering from something that causes my one side to drag and they can't find any reason. Another member of our group, Katherine, is suffering from the exact same thing I am, but you go to the doctor and they can't find any reason. I may be three miles from the mining site. I can feel tremors when they set off blasts.

Cary: The city of Amstead goes up to the top of the mountain. If you get up on top and look down in the next valley, that's where they're blasting. It's that close to Amstead, okay? There's old mine tunnels there. I don't know where they are, but people say they worked in them. So when these blasting operations go to work, they will be over top of some of these tunnels—mines, you know. Now, is there a water problem? It all depends on how they take that water out of there. I've been in the mines quite a long time, and it seems to me like if the top has fell in and there's headwater in the tunnels and they go to blasting again, Amstead might get a bath.

Beverly: That was one of the things that was brought up at a meeting, and the DEP guy said, "If it's not on my map, it's not there."

Delilah: When we flew over Charleston with the tour, there are two huge sites right over the river. I saw that and I thought, I'm not an engineer. My daddy was a coal miner, and I know absolutely nothing about this stuff. But even I've got better sense than that. You don't blow off the mountaintop and put a poison slurry right over your river. That makes no sense.

James: They always use all our water systems as waste. It looks like they're going right along the river now, while they can. They know it's gonna stop sooner or later. And they try to get what they don't think they can get in the future. They're getting it now, and then they don't have to worry about it. I've actually seen a few mining companies that say in ten years they're gonna switch back to deep mining. So they know it's gonna get harder for 'em to get permits.

Cary: If I go out here to start a business and I have to have money to start that business, and I go out here to the bank, they don't want to know what I'm going to do next year. They want to know what you're going to do and your projections for this. You've got to have a business plan, okay. So why can't the coal companies be held to the same standards? When they fire up the first permit, it should be a matter of public record that we can go see where the next permit is and when it's gonna start and how far it's gonna continue in the future so that we know what's gonna happen to our area. If your child goes and gets a job with the coal company, does he have two years or does he have twenty years? They know, but they just don't let the information out. It's the old thing of divide and conquer. If we put you all out there, not only are we affecting Amstead, but we're gonna affect

Summersville and all these other areas. (If they know ahead of time), all these people are gonna get fired up and come in and say, "Hey, you're tearing up everything." So as long as it's just one little area, there's only a few people that's gonna create a disturbance. They can deal with that, okay. Once we get through on the Amstead part and go to Summersville, Amstead people's gonna back off. They know that. So they've already tore mine up—why should I go help Summersville when they didn't help me? That's exactly what they're doing.

James: They just know that if it ain't in your backyard, you're just gonna forget about it. I'm not going to forget about it—the way they treated me.

Karen: This is the front yard. The rest of the state is the backyard. If everybody started thinking of it that a way, they'd think about what's coming.

Beverly: Another thing is that they'll publish a permit in one paper, and then the next permit they'll publish in another paper. So you have to take all these papers and read every paper. We all thought the DEP was protecting us. We didn't realize that they were protecting the coal companies and not us.

Cary: The DEP has to go by the way the laws are written. If the coal companies go by the laws, the DEP has to give them that permit. If you have a federal inspector come in, he's going to go by federal guideline, okay. When the next cycle comes around and we get a different inspector, he'll go to the same book and you'd think it's the same thing. But no, this is not right; you have to change it. So, the laws are made to where it's the way you interpret the law—who's the man doing the interpreting, you see. That's the way I think they get around the DEP.

James: There's so many loopholes in the law. They've got all these words, like "feasible." They'll say things like, "It's not 'feasible' to treat this water."

Beverly: Well, if they start blowing up that mountain up there, depending on how the weather is this year. If it's wet weather, then all that stuff's not going to go into the air, but it's going to go into the streams. If it's dry weather when they do the blasting, then it's going to go into the air and it's going to go everywhere. So then you're going to deal with the streams, the animals, the environment, the people. The people all around are the ones who are going to be the ones to suffer, because I'd say if you lined ten of us up in a row, eight of them would have no health insurance. So anything that comes about from this silica that's in the air, the selenium in the water, the minerals that's going places it shouldn't go, the toxic waste, all the fuel that they bring in, all the oil they bring in (what's going to happen then?) going into the dirt, washing down to our waters, washing down to our gardens, washing down to our vegetables that's supposed to be good for us—a big bowl of toxic waste. Any way you go, it's not going to be good.

James: This guy said, "Oh, well, we put these chemicals in there to treat the water. They say the metals drop down to the bottom and the clean water runs off the top." And me and my wife said, "Where do you think those metals go. They don't go nowhere. They stay in that pond, unless you want to pump 'em out and then you take 'em somewhere and put 'em somewhere else. You're not really getting rid of it. You're just taking it from here to here; then, if you gotta take it from here, you gotta move it back over here. It's getting in the earth some way."

Cary: I believe they're changing, too, going from these ponds to what they call "sediment ditches." It looks to me like that's just another way of getting around the pond. If they blast out, they send that down over the mountain, so instead of one big spill like we had at Buffalo Creek,

every time we get a big rain, we're going to have wash somewhere outside this mountain. And it may be different communities that's affected. But what it all boils down to is it's going to be in all the water that's below there. So whatever river runs below it, somewhere it's going to get to that river. The Kanawa goes to the Ohio; the Ohio goes to the Mississippi; the Mississippi goes to the Gulf. Everything on this side—half the United States—is going to be affected.

James: They don't realize that if it started up here, they'd better pay attention.

Cary: What's really happening right here, if they blast the tops of the mountains off and they fill the streams in below and they take our water where there is none—down in Atlanta last year they were almost in crisis mode, okay? Where does the New River head up at? It ends up in North Carolina. So what's to prevent North Carolina from saying, "Hey, boys, I'm going to build a dam." If that happens, that cuts us off—we're high and dry. We don't have any water from the New River and we don't have any for our houses cause we've plugged it off—we've filled it up. Right now we have one of the best water tables in the United States. We have three things: we have coal, we have water, and we have natural beauty. They're getting rid of all three of 'em.

James: And timber. I don't care what they say about putting it back, it don't grow. I'd rather see them do contour mining than what they do now. I mean, it looks like crap, but they did get trees to grow. But none of the trees are like that now. They're stunted. But that one area (the reclamation demonstration park), I guarantee they've spent so much money on soil—bringing in top soil to get all that to grow so they could have something to hang their hats on. "Look," they say, "we've planted a million trees over here." But look how many billion they tore down before they planted them million, though.

Beverly: If they were doing all this in the Rain Forest, people would be outraged. They're doing it right here in our country. One thing the coal does when it's in that mountain—it purifies the water; the rain water drains down through the coal. That's what's giving us all the clean drinking water. Once you take that coal out, we're not going to have anymore clean drinking water. A lot of water filters use bituminous coal, so it stands to reason that coal is in the mountains for a reason. It purifies the water. So what are we going to do when the coal's gone?

Karen: That's the reason so many communities around here got their water supply from old mines, and they didn't have to use chemicals in it to make it useful. It was already pure. We don't drink city water. We filter it before we drink it.

Cary: It really tickled me: the other day one of your guys came in, and he had taken a water sample. He came in and set a bottle up on a stand and said, "This is Crapichino." And that's what it looked like.

Patricia: I'm curious about what got you all involved. A lot of people see the big problem, but so few people say, "Hey, I'm gonna do something."

Beverly: There was this line that was going to go in, and they were going to bring the coal trucks down through the town and make this hairpin turn in front of the head-start building. We didn't want coal trucks coming down by the head-start building cause if they lose brakes or something, they'd go right through the head-start building. And we got involved that way. That stopped about the same time this other permit was starting up, and the more we looked at this permit, the more problems we seen with it. And the more questions we asked, the more we wouldn't get any answers. And that's how we got involved. A couple of years ago, I wouldn't have known a lot of this stuff.

Karen: The thing that really infuriated us, too, was the very fact that we had been working for several years to clean up the town of Amstead. It's an original coal town. All or most of the houses are old coal camps. But people have cleaned up and fixed up and done everything in their beings to make things better for everyone, to look at, to live there, to bring their children back home—because so many of them left after high school. Now they don't have anything to come back to again if they're going to start doing the same thing they had before. If we keep things going like they're going, keeping it clean, the tourist industry has got to bring in more money than the coal companies. The coal companies take the money out, but where does it go? I don't see it, and I'm sure that none of the rest of them see it. They don't put anything back into the communities. They don't fix anything when they leave. They don't give us anything to be proud of.

Beverly: You know, it's not the miners that are coming in, keeping my business going. It's the tourists. And the local people.

James: I believe that's where my future is—with the rafters and the tourism and stuff like that.

Cary: I grew up in Amstead—that was home. The town was a bustling little community. I mean we had a Krogers store, an IGA store, a meat market, a lot of people, a lot of coal miners. But they were deep miners. Their money went into the stores. We had everything there. It was a coal town. It was dirty. But we had a ball field. And the coal miners would build the fence and mow the grass so they could play in that ball field when they had time off. Once the coal companies moved, the children left. There was no pride. They didn't want to come back because it was dirty. Now the people, in the last fifteen years or so, are beginning to take pride again. They're mowing their grass, painting their houses. Now, what happens, just when you get your head above water, here comes the coal company, and the town is back down to what it was. And I just don't think that's right. I mean, we don't want to keep the people from making a living with coal mining, but we don't want them to tear up what we've got, either.

James: Yeah, you fight for what you've got, and then they just knock it down for you—you don't have it no more.

Cary: Why should one man get rich and a hundred people go broke? It's just not right.

Karen: Amstead's now a Blue-Print Community. What's going to happen with that?

Cary: That's awarded by the Governor. Amstead was chosen because we have that much more on the ball. In other words, people are beginning to try to make a difference. Not only are we a Blue-Print Community and recognized by the state and given money and a chance to get more money, but we have the New River, a national river, running down one side of this town, and six miles from that river we have the Gauley River Recreational Area. So we're sitting right dead in the middle. That's a boon for tourism.

Beverly: And that's where that coal mine's sitting.

Cary: And it's going to take the mountains off that's between those two meccas for tourism. It makes no sense at all.

James: And how many new rafting companies? I mean, there's so much going on.

Cary: Seventeen, eighteen, nineteen rafting companies.

Beverly: And housing developments.

Cary: Thirty-five hundred new homes coming down on one side of the river, okay, and six-hundred and some coming up the other side. So why do we want to keep tearing up the mountains when we're drawing the people here?

Patricia: So what have you all tried so far? Where are you in the fight?

Cary: Well, we have wrote letters and sent petitions to Rockefeller, Rahall, Bird, and Mansion. I got an instant response from Rockefeller. Bird said, "That's a local issue. I don't have time to fool with it." I got an instant thing from Governor Mansion, said he turned it over to the DEP. That's the blind leading the blind.

Beverly: Well, Mansion and Rahall, and Rockefeller are Friends of Coal.

Cary: I've published two letters in the Gazette and the Tribune, and out of that we've had people contact us and say, "How do we get involved?" So it does help. And some of these people have come to the meetings. But the newspapers will edit your letters.

James: Yeah, they did mine, too. It burned me up. I sent mine to the Sinclair Broadcasting, too. If any of 'em bother me, I let 'em know about it now. I'll send it to anyone who wants to listen, and if they don't want to listen, I'll send it anyway. I'll say, "You're gonna listen."

Karen: And we sent packages to ABC, NBC, and CBS.

Cary: We've got people working in New York who can maybe get us something to Michael Moore, and maybe he'll do a documentary on it. One thing we need, and maybe you all can help us: if we can get the NAACP involved—because most of these people who were killed in the tunnel was Black people. If we could get Jesse Jackson or Stapleton in here and get national exposure, people would sit up and take notice.

Beverly: I think that's our problem. We haven't been able to dig our heels in on national exposure.

Cary: Yeah, see, Larry Gibson has got exposure drawn into his part of the country.

Beverly: But it's not stopping them.

Patricia: When Larry started, he was on his own.

James: Yeah, nineteen years ago.

Patricia: And it's just now gathering national momentum.

Beverly: There's a very good movie coming out, called *Burning the Future: Coal in America*.

James: With the coal companies, I think they have so much money that it's hard to put pressure on people that's got that much pressure on them, too.

Beverly: But the people, themselves, are scared to death.

James: I call it gutless. I hate to say it, but we're gutless. We want to just sit back and let them handle it.

Cary: I got kids and grandkids and a bunch of greats. When you're working for a company and you're told to quit your job for something like this, and then you go home and your kids or grandkids say, "Can I have this?" Guess who you're going to listen to. That's what it amounts to.

James: They don't realize that, for the future, if you don't stop, that grandkid ain't gonna have nothing. That's the thing.

Cary: We have to go at it a different way. We have to get people to come and look to see what we've got out here. See, when I worked in the mines, I saw what I worked at every day, but I didn't get to see the whole picture. Nobody ever gets to see the whole big picture until someone makes a movie.

Beverly: It's not the people's fault. It's the people that controls things that create this.

Karen: It's a shame that we can't even take our grandkids fishing and catch a fish and bring it home and cook it.

Beverly: What fish?

James: You watch the Gauley here pretty soon. It's gonna be hurting. I know it is.

Beverly: I think the citizens that are having the impact put upon them need to take control over some of the testing [water] to make sure that what they're seeing is being read right.

Patricia: You know one resource that we were talking about just today is the DMR report, "The Discharge Monitoring Report." Any company that gets a permit to discharge something into water has to issue a DMR report monthly, on what they're putting into the water. They're not even bothering to lie anymore.

Cary: I think national attention has to happen. We have to get people who live out of state on our side. We need educated people, like the professor from the University of Tennessee, who said, "One blown-up mountain equals one hour of electricity." How many mountains have we got? It's not worth the price, people. Coal's a good thing, but you have to use it in the right way. You don't to tear up more good than what coal can replace, okay? Liquefied coal's not going to help because then you use up two resources at the same time.

Beverly: I think they have to do away with mountaintop removal, period, and stay with deep mining.

Cary: They can do this with a high-wall miner. They take eight or nine feet at a time, and they get all the coal. They don't have to blast the mountains off. We've still got our natural beauty. We've still got our timber.

James: That's what I don't understand, why they have to take the whole mountain just for that little bit.

Beverly: Every time we go up there, there's another mountain stripped. It's devastating just to go up there and look at it and see nothing but barren land. Then you look over a little further and you see where they've dumped the garbage over the hillside. Then you see all these blasting areas. Then you look down over the hill, and there's that stream disappearing. And you see life is disappearing. Rip, rape, and run.

photo by Vivian Stockman

Kayford Mountain, West Virginia

Destruction

by Kayla K. Ward

It was the destruction of the land
that brought the rain this year.

It stormed and the stadium shook empty.

Empty skies, empty shelves
Empty tolls, empty hands

Empty lanes on the highway
in the rain where we took
joyrides in abandoned buggies.

We pushed and pushed and
laughed until we broke the wheels off.

We screamed along with the
scraping metal on asphalt
until crows cawed into our nightmares.

We threw rocks into jagged glass windows
and hit every letter in WALMART
except for the first two and next to last.

The door sign still read "Open All Holidays"
and everything left stranded had been eaten
by the opossum-rats.

We snickered with our black teeth,
watched them wait for us to walk
through the doors.

We kicked aluminum cans and
imagined the plastic bags caught in
whirlwind and soot taking us with them.

This Land is God's Land

lyrics by Kayla Ward
© 2008 *Kathleen Coffee*

Verse 1
Five-thousand feet under the earth
Digging for diamonds, digging for mirth
Digging for days when the water and sand
Would carry them bones back to God's land

Like a black-out in a miner's coal town
Where women shed their blood to poverty bound
And whiskey kept them warm and working for the man
Safe distances away from reaching God's land

Chorus
But mercy does not budge
For the deadliest of sludge
Taking everything we own
Except for our souls alone

Verse 2
Five-thousand feet under the earth
Burying secrets of a digger man's curse
And holding a gun the size of God's hand
To blow and throw loud sounds into a government

Band-wagon of war
Destroying families to the core
Caused by five thousand years of dynamite hands
Digging for diamonds in God's land

Chorus
But mercy does not budge
For the deadliest of sludge
Taking everything we own
Except for our souls alone

Chanting
This is God's Land
Oh five-thousand feet
This Land is God's Land
Oh five-thousand years
Digging, Digging
In sepulchers on the Earth
It is God's Land

Buffalo Creek remembered— Feb 27, 2007

Survivor recalls horrifying moments, haunting memories

by Ken Ward, Jr.

originally published in *The Charleston Gazette*

Thirty-five years to the day after he narrowly escaped death at Buffalo Creek, memories of the disaster still haunt Arley Johnson.

Johnson, his mother and eight brothers and sisters scrambled up a hillside just minutes before a wall of water and coal waste hit their Amherstdale home.

"I had time to get a pair of pants on, a blanket and a pair of boots," Johnson, who was 12 at the time, recalled Monday afternoon.

A lot of Johnson's neighbors weren't so fortunate.

Shortly before 8 a.m. on Feb. 26, 1972, a Pittston Coal slurry dam far up Buffalo Creek collapsed. More than 132 million gallons of water and coal waste rushed down the hollow from Saunders to Man.

By the time the flood was over, 125 people had died. Another 1,100 were injured and about 4,000 were left homeless.

On Monday afternoon, about 75 people gathered at the state Capitol to commemorate the 35th anniversary of the Buffalo Creek disaster.

The Rev. Dennis Sparks, executive director of the West Virginia Council of Churches, said the event was held "lest we forget the agony that was brought on so many people" by the disaster.

In a low-key event just outside the House chamber, organizers showed several videos with footage of the disaster's aftermath. A handful of environmental and labor lobbyists stopped by, and only a few lawmakers attended.

Johnson, a former delegate, gave the keynote address, calling Buffalo Creek "a great watershed event" for himself and for West Virginia.

Five years after Buffalo Creek, lawmakers repeatedly cited the disaster when they passed the landmark Surface Mine Control and Reclamation Act of 1977 to force federal regulation of strip mining.

For example, one committee report noted Buffalo Creek in explaining why state and federal inspectors needed authority to shut down mining operations that posed imminent danger to public safety or the environment.

"To provide otherwise would be to perpetrate the possibility of tragedies such as the Buffalo Creek flood, which can be at least partially attributed to the sad fact that government regulation of the collapsed mine waste banks fell between the cracks of the not quite meshed functions of state and federal agencies," said the House committee report from April 1977.

Johnson recalled that Pittston Coal officials knew that the dam was reaching the breaking point, and that government officials all the way up to then-Gov. Arch Moore had been warned of the danger.

"My government failed me, and failed my classmates and failed my siblings," Johnson said.

Johnson recalled going to a makeshift morgue in a local school, seeing the body of a child his age, and trying to wipe the mud off her face. "She was a classmate of mine," Johnson said. "We were square dance partners."

"The water was very black," he said. "It was nasty. It was sludge.

"That day, every victim was the same color—they were all black," Johnson said. "They were black in their hair. It was grimy. It was slimy. It was nasty."

Today, hundreds of coal-waste dams still dot the Appalachian coalfields.

Regulators and the coal industry say these dams are much different from the one that failed at Buffalo Creek. Modern coal dams are designed and built to detailed engineering specifications, they say. Dams are regularly inspected, they say, and enforcement is tough.

But in October 2000, the floor fell out of Massey Energy's Big Branch Impoundment in Martin County, Kentucky. More than 300 million gallons of slurry—28 times larger than the Exxon Valdez oil spill—poured into an adjacent underground mine. From there, the slurry flowed out into two local streams and into the Tug Fork of the Big Sandy River, along the West Virginia-Kentucky border.

Lawns were buried up to seven feet deep, and all of the fish were killed in two streams. Drinking water supplies were fouled along more than 60 miles of the Big Sandy.

After Martin County, the National Academy of Sciences said in an October 2001 report that tougher regulation of slurry dams was needed. But neither the federal Office of Surface Mining nor the Mine Safety and Health Administration has issued new impoundment rules.

And concern over coal slurry disposal continues.

At Monday's event, some Raleigh County residents said they still worry about a Massey Energy impoundment just upstream from Marsh Fork Elementary School. Six years before Buffalo Creek, a dam collapsed near the mining village of Aberfan in South Wales, killing 144 people, including 116 children at a school below the impoundment.

Also, residents of Mingo County are concerned that a nearby impoundment, along with the injection of slurry underground—touted by the National Academy as a possible alternative to dams—is polluting their drinking water.

Johnson, who now works for the governor's Office of Economic Opportunity, said he tried to work to address such concerns when he was in the Legislature.

"How is it that we can live in a state that is so wealthy in resources, in water and natural gas and coal, and our people still be so poor?" Johnson said.

Reclamation

by Rhonda Browning White

Papaw called it a welcome ugly sight—
her mountains bleeding black rivers.
It means food on miners' tables tonight,
payment to company store upriver.

Her mountains bleeding black rivers,
her heart hacked open to haul a ton of soul—
payment to company store upriver,
more wealth for Pittston and Consolidated Coal.

Her heart hacked open to haul a ton of soul,
holes gouged like dark eyes into black depths,
more wealth for Pittston and Consolidated Coal.
She reclaimed Buffalo Creek the day the skies wept,

holes gouged like dark eyes into black depths.
Raped again, and again, her mercy now gone,
she reclaimed Buffalo Creek the day the skies wept.
A black river named Bluestone, the place I called home,

raped again, and again, her mercy now gone.
She'll take it all back, one house at a time,
a black river named Bluestone, the place I called home;
houses washed away—one that was mine.

She'll take it all back, one house at a time,
bottomland neighborhoods covered in gray snow.
Houses washed away—one that was mine;
we'll build it right back, 'cause it's all we know.

Bottomland neighborhoods covered in gray snow,
Papaw called it a welcome ugly sight.
We'll build it right back, 'cause it's all we know
It means food on miners' tables tonight.

photo by Kent Kessinger

Appalachian Waterfall

West Virginia: Forward and Back

by Rhonda Browning White

I.

Mountaineers, miners—
broken hearts and bare hills.

Men moving mountains,
clear-cut timber,
black-bleeding Earth sliced open.

This slaughtered land—"progress."

II.

Progress?
Land slaughtered,
this open-sliced Earth bleeding black,
timber cut clear.

Mountains moving men:
hills bare and hearts broken—
miners,
mountaineers.

The Twilight of Twilight?

by Michael E. Workman, Jr.

I've lived in Twilight, WV, my whole life. It used to be a booming town. Now, it's scary just thinking about getting out of your house and going down the road. Mountaintop removal operations practically surround us. Our air is choked with dust from the blasting and hillsides seem unstable. Sludge ponds, too, are releasing nasty chemicals into our environment. It seems like a lot of people are sick with breathing problems, or have cancer and are dying.

Coal trucks hog the road and drag piles of mud off the mining sites onto the road. The mounds of mud have caused bad accidents.

Many of us living here don't feel safe—and it's not just the chemicals and dangerous roads, it's also the worry about flooding coming off the mangled mountains. People have been driven away; those of us left want to keep our birthright. But what will be left for our children and grandchildren?

The coal companies have no right to bully and threaten those of us who dare to speak out about what they are doing to our land and our futures! We want jobs—but we want jobs that don't poison our families—jobs with a future.

Let the coal bosses come live in Twilight. Let them wake up during a rainstorm, in a panic, wondering if this time the floods will come. Let them hear the doctor say, no it isn't asthma, but dust from the mines that's causing your breathing problems. Maybe then the coal bosses would support the proud people fighting for what is right.

But probably not—they sure don't care about the workers they are trying to turn against us, or the communities they are destroying.

All they care about is making a quick buck, no matter the trail of devastation they leave behind.

Like the Mountains Richly Veined

by Marianne Worthington, Williamsburg, KY

*Text of a Reading delivered at Church of the Savior,
United Church of Christ, Knoxville, Tennessee, Jan 22, 2006*

My name is Marianne Worthington, and I've been welcomed by this assembly as a visitor in this church on many occasions. Because I was brought up in the music of the church and have, off and on, served as a church musician for over 30 years, I have especially enjoyed the witness of your music ministry. In this church I've heard sacred and secular music, jazz, folk, and pop, gospel, and contemporary Christian music, offered up always to the Glory of God. Along with your commitments to spiritual growth through activities that foster social equality and sustainable communities, your musical engagements demonstrate to me that you are a fair-minded people, tolerant, and sweet, who love each other and your community.

In thinking about what I could say to you today about the disgraceful mining practice of mountaintop removal, I kept returning to your music ministry which led me to the place where I have always found my faith and where I continue to gain spiritual strength: the hymnbook

I grew up in Central Baptist Church of Fountain City where I absorbed the rich music and poetry of traditional hymns. As a child I learned by heart many of the hymns that have nature themes: "For the Beauty of the Earth," "This Is My Father's World," "All Things Bright and Beautiful." And I sang them without paying too much attention, but I realize now that those songs, that I had learned in the church, helped me to see the wonders of nature, helped me to formulate a moral imperative of good stewardship of the earth.

The father of English hymnody, Isaac Watts wrote this hymn nearly 300 years ago:

> We sing your mighty power, O God,
> that made the mountains rise,
> Oh how your wonders are displayed,

> wherever we turn our eyes
> If we survey the ground we tread,
> or gaze upon the skies.

Today, we have not so many opportunities to witness nature's wonders from the mountains' rise in southeastern Kentucky, where I now live, or in the mountains of Virginia, West Virginia, and Tennessee. The scale of ecological destruction caused by mountaintop removal mining is unfathomable, frightening, heartbreaking. For instance, nearly a half million acres of Appalachian hardwood forests have been clear cut to make way for mountaintop removal, and the mining companies don't even attempt to salvage the timber. It goes down the side of a mountain with the rest of what the mining companies call the "overburden," usually into streams or valleys below.

In 1923, a Methodist minister from Kentucky, Thomas Obediah Chisholm, wrote this hymn:

> Summer and winter and springtime and harvest
> Sun, moon and stars in their courses above
> join with all nature in manifold witness
> to God's great faithfulness, mercy and love.
> Great is Thy faithfulness, . . .
> morning by morning new mercies I see.

I wonder what Thomas Chisholm would think about his Kentucky now, where morning by morning many residents experience not new mercies, but omnipresent noise, air pollution from mining dust and debris, buried waterways, mountain vistas irreparably altered, and the ruination of plant and wildlife habitats. A Kentucky where coal companies engaged in mountaintop removal have hundreds of coal sludge ponds where they store the byproduct of processing coal for energy use. This slurry—a toxic tar-like substance—contains arsenic, mercury, lead, and copper. When one of these ponds failed in Inez, Kentucky, in 2000, the slurry killed aquatic life for 70 miles, contaminated ground water, and wrecked homes, businesses, schools, and churches. The mining company argued in court that the slurry spill was "an act of God."

Could the Swedish pastor and politician Carl Gustaf Boberg have foreseen the irony in what has become the great ecumenical and international hymn he penned in 1885?

> When I look down from lofty mountain grandeur
> and hear the brook, and feel the gentle breeze;
> Then sings my soul, my Savior God to thee;
> how great thou art.

The lofty mountain grandeur is fast disappearing in our part of Appalachia. The flattened mountaintops have variously been described as looking like: highways on a lunar landscape, a once beautiful animal with a debilitating case of mange, and shelves of rock that are jagged, scarred, pocked. What were once pristine mountain ranges now resemble the harsh tablelands of the desert southwest.

In contemporary hymn books, we still have these traditional hymns in praise of nature, but what we also have are many hymns that implore God to forgive us for our devastating and destructive practices toward nature. Consider the hymn of United Church of Christ pastor and hymn writer Ruth Duck:

> Forgive us for each flower and bird
> now vanished by our hand.
> Teach us to treat with loving care
> the creatures of the land.
> Forgive us that we threaten sea and air.
> Teach us to tend life's fragile web
> with wise and tender care.

Or David Mehrtens' hymn titled "The World Abounds"

> Give thanks for plains and valleys
> paced by mountains thrusting high
> Give thanks by fighting greed and waste
> that drain their treasure dry

Or the hymn of the ecumenical and well-known hymnist, Brian Wren.

> We thank you, God, for minerals and ores,
> the basis of all building, wealth, and speed.
> Forgive our reckless plundering and waste.
> Help us renew the face of the earth.

The focus in Christian hymnody has shifted from admiring and extolling nature to taking responsibility for the natural world our creator bestowed on us and entrusted to our care. All of these hymns continue to reinforce my responsibility as a steward of the earth.

I turn to the hymnbook because when I turn to mining officials, I find no solace, and certainly no answers. The Office of Surface Mining, part of our government's Department of the Interior, is charged with protecting the environment during coal mining and making sure the land is reclaimed afterward. But when I looked at the Frequently Asked Questions on their website, I was alarmed that they take no responsibility for mountaintop removal mining:

> *Question:* What are the benefits of mountaintop removal compared to deep mining?
> *Answer:* The Office of Surface Mining doesn't have information comparing the benefits of different mining techniques.
> *Question:* Underground coal mining seems to have less environmental impacts than mountaintop removal mining, so why is it being used instead?
> *Answer:* The Office of Surface Mining doesn't govern the decisions to mine a particular coal deposit and the technique by which it is mined. This question is best answered by the mining industry or mining associations.

So I went to the mining associations. The West Virginia Coal Association calls Mountaintop removal mining a "temporary disruption." And the Kentucky Coal Association claims this type of coal mining does not eliminate or block streams, that erosion of a mountainside does not contribute to flooding, that mountaintop removal improves habitats for wildlife in Kentucky, and that once a site is reclaimed, it still looks like a mountain. "What's left is flatter, more useful land on the *top* of the mountain."

Who will take responsibility for the people killed in Appalachia due to flooding, mudslides, rockslides, flying debris, speeding and overloaded coal trucks—all consequences of mountaintop removal mining?

Who will take responsibility for speaking with elected officials our shock and fear of losing another ecosystem and for many of us, our mountain culture and heritage?

Who will take responsibility for finding and demanding alternative energy sources?

Of course, it must be us as a body of believers, as keepers of each other, as stewards of the earth.

In 1985, the Presbyterian theologian and poet Thomas Troeger penned the hymn "God Folds the Mountains Out of Rock." I want to share his poignant warning as a benediction:

> God folds the mountains out of rock
> and fuses elemental powers
> in ores and atoms we unlock
> to claim as if their wealth were ours.
> From veins of stone we lift up fire,
> and too impressed by our own skill
> we use the flame that we acquire,
> not thinking of the Maker's will.
>
> Our instruments can probe and sound
> the folded mountain's potent core
> but wisdom's ways are never found
> among the lodes of buried ore.
> Yet wisdom is the greater need,
> and wisdom is the greatest source,
> for lacking wisdom we proceed
> to waste God's other gifts.
>
> Lord, grant us what we cannot mine,
> what science cannot plumb or chart—
> your wisdom and your truth divine
> enfolded in a faithful heart.
> Then we like mountains richly veined
> will be a source of light and flame
> whose energies have been ordained
> to glorify the Maker's name.
>
> Amen.

Works cited —

Baptist Hymnal. Nashville, TN: Genevox Press, 1991
Chalice Hymnal. Atlanta, GA: Chalice Press, 2002.
Clines, Francis X. "And Now to 'Streamline' King Coal's Beheading of Appalachia." *New York Times.* 7 Nov 2005.
<http://www.nytimes.com/2005/11/07/opinion/07mon3.html>
"The Cost of Coal." *NOW with Bill Moyers* (transcript). 2 Aug 2002.
<http://www.pbs.org/now/transcript/transcript_coal.html>
"Environmental Impacts of MTR." *Appalachian Voices.* 2002.<http://www.appvoices.org/mtr/mtr_ei.asp>
House, Silas. "Saving a Mountain." *Appalachian Life.* Aug/Sept 2002: 10-12.
Johannsen, Kristin, Bobbie Ann Mason, and Mary Ann Taylor-Hall, eds. *Missing Mountains: We Went to the Mountaintop but It Wasn't There.* Nicholasville, KY: Wind, 2005.
"Katuah Earth First! Blockades Mountain Top Removal Site on Zeb Mountain in Campbell County, TN." *Tennessee Independent Media Center.*
<http://www.tnimc.org/feature/display/547/index.php>
Lydersen, Kari. "Resisting Mountaintop Removal in Tennessee." *The NewStandard.* 21 Nov 2005.
<http://www.alternet.org/story/28489>
"Mountaintop Mining." *Kentucky Coal Association.* 2001.
<http://www.kentuckycoal.com/>
"Mountaintop Removal Mining: Frequently Asked Questions." *Office of Surface Mining.* 11 April 2005.
<http://www.osmre.gov/mountaintopfaq.htm>
"Myths and Facts." *Appalachian Voices.* 2002.
<http://www.appvoices.org/mtr/mtr_mythsfacts.asp>
A New Century Hymnal. Cleveland, OH: Pilgrim Press, 1996.
Pancake, Ann. "Power Out: Middle-Class Privilege, Working-Class Paradox and Who Pays the Electric Bill in Contemporary America." *Push Magazine.* 2003.
<http://www.pushmagazine.org/Push/article6.html>
The Presbyterian Hymnal. Louisville, KY: Westminster/John Knox Press, 1990
Reece, Erik. "Death of a Mountain: Radical strip mining and the leveling of Appalachia." *Harper's.* April, 2005: 41-60.

___. *Lost Mountain: A Year in the Vanishing Wilderness. Radical Strip Mining and the Devastation of Appalachia.* New York: Riverhead Books, 2006.

___. "Moving Mountains. The battle for justice comes to the coal fields of Appalachia." *Orion Magazine.* Jan/Feb 2006. <http://www.oriononline.org/pages/om/06-1om/Reece.html>

West Virginia Coal Association. http://www.wvcoal.com/.